Father Pat:
A Hero of the Far West

Mrs. Jerome Mercier

DODO ☉ PRESS

Father Pat
A Hero of the Far West
By Mrs. Jerome Mercier

With a Preface by
The Right Reverend John Dart, D.D.

1909.

NOTICE

THIS year, 1909, is the Jubilee Year of the Church of England in British Columbia. For on S. Matthias' Day, February the twenty-fourth, 1859, the good Bishop Hills was consecrated to the oversight of that vast province, now divided into four dioceses (Columbia, Caledonia, New Westminster, and Kootenay, the two last as yet under one Bishop). It seems a fitting time, therefore, to put forth a short record of the brave life of one who was a hero to his flock, a Father Dolling of the West, the Reverend Henry Irwin, known far and wide in British Columbia as "Father Pat." The memoir has been compiled, with the aid of many kind friends, at the request of the Bishop of New Westminster and Kootenay, and after a visit to the places where the memory of Father Pat is still beloved and cherished.

ANNE MERCIER.
KEMERTON, February 1909.

PREFACE

THE life of a missionary priest in Canada amongst settlers is not often an eventful one. It generally presents a record of hard, monotonous work like that of a poor priest in a scattered agricultural parish in England. There are, however, some points of difference. The Canadian priest must cover much longer distances both walking and riding, and he must be more frequently away from home. He should, therefore, be decidedly hardy and athletic. Again, he has to deal with a greater variety of people than can be found in an old-world parish. Besides those born in the Dominion, immigrants from Britain, Scandinavia, Italy, and the States, some ignorant, others well educated, will all be met with in his travels. If these men have reason to believe that the missionary is a true and sympathetic man, they will attend his services and be inclined to follow his lead. Cecil's remark applies to British Columbia even more forcibly than it does to England: "Men look to a man out of the pulpit, to see what he is worth in it."

It was because Henry Irwin always showed himself to be unselfish, sympathetic, and anxious to help others to the very utmost of his power, that he won Ins great influence amongst the pioneers of British Columbia and that his name and memory are held by them in affection and respect. Stories showing his character are often told, e.g. how he went to a man who had been injured by an accident, and drew him in a sledge over the snow several miles to his home; how he would carry the consolations of religion in stormy weather up the mountains to sick miners, in spite of the opposition (not confined to words) of the thoughtless and godless in the vicinity. Manners and customs have become more polished in British Columbia than they were in early days. A dialogue like the following would scarcely be possible now during service, even in the newest and roughest camps. A minister is interrupted in a prayer for a person by a miner with all gravity, and with no intentional irreverence. "Hold up, parson, I don't pray for that fellow." "Why not?" "Because the papers say so and so about him." "Well, but the papers don't always speak the truth, do they?" "Not by a long chalk," was the reply.

"And if all these stories were true, he would need our prayers all the more, wouldn't he?" "Well, I guess you are right, parson; fire away."

Soon after I arrived in British Columbia, in 1895, Henry Irwin wrote to me from his living in the north of Ireland, offering his services to the diocese.

Rossland was then rising into notice as a mining camp, and Irwin, who had been missionary at Golden, and afterwards chaplain to Bishop Sillitoe, seemed, from the reports that reached me, to be just the man for the place. Accordingly he was sent there, and the result answered my expectations. Very soon a spacious frame building was erected for a church, with rooms in the basement to serve as a lodging for the priest and a club for the men in the neighbourhood. But I do not remember ever finding Irwin in his own rooms. They were always giving shelter to poor .people who had been reduced to want, whilst he himself had a shake-down in some friendly bachelor's "shack." Nor was he unmindful of the wider interests of the Church, as he showed by taking a prominent part in the measures that led to the erection of Kootenay into a separate Diocese. When Rossland became more civilized and comparatively rich, Irwin left it to take up pioneer work in the neighbouring boundary country. Here he remained until his health imperatively demanded rest and change. We were all hoping he would return to us in renewed health and strength after a short visit to his friends in Ireland; but God saw fit to order it otherwise. *Beatus mortuus.*

JOHN, NEW WESTMINSTER AND KOOTENAY.

CHAPTER I
HOME AND SCHOOL LIFE

ON August 2nd, 1859, was born among the Wicklow Mountains a bright, happy, Irish boy, full of life and fun Henry Irwin, one of a family belonging to the old Church School of Ireland. His father was incumbent of Newtown, Mount Kennedy, from 1863 to 1894, and his grandfather was Precentor of Armagh Cathedral, and Chaplain and Secretary to the Primate, Archbishop Beresford. His great-grandfather was Archdeacon of Emly.

Thus we see that Church feeling was innate in him, and his merry, brave boyish spirit, far from lessening this feeling, only added ardour to it. When a mere child his saying was: "I am going to be a missionary."

In the roomy old family house, "Prospect House," in view of the Wicklow Mountains, Henry Irwin received his first lessons from a lady; who speaks of his sweet and affectionate disposition, willing to share his toys and pleasures, never bearing malice or sullen after punishment. "To do *something* was a necessity to him," she says; he entered into all boyish games with zest, and loved all animals, horses especially. He was a fearless rider, and scoured the country on his shaggy pony. His brother observes: "I believe it was this rough riding in his boyhood that fitted Henry so well for the work to which he afterwards devoted his life. All through his school and college life he studied to train and harden his body in all kinds of manly exercises, always with the one end in view."

At the age of twelve Henry Irwin went to S. Columba's School, intended to be a sort of Irish Eton, of which Dr. Sewell, the brother of the authoress and headmaster of S. Peter's College, Radley, was one of the founders. Archbishop Beresford, Bishop Moberly, Archbishop Magee, and A. J. Beresford Hope were also promoters of this school, which was founded in 1843. When young Irwin went to school, S. Columba's had migrated to Holly Lodge, Co. Dublin. From its

1

earliest days the school had a fine *esprit de corps*, and impressed its pupils with earnest zeal for the Church.

The Rev. R. Rice, Principal of S. Columba's when Henry Irwin was a pupil there, has kindly sent me the following details:

"Henry Irwin was the eldest of four brothers, of whom three were educated at S. Columba's College, and three of these four have done good work as missionaries. From the first Henry showed high and strong principle, ever ready with his work, ever near the front in the playfield, ever attentive and devout in chapel. These traits became more distinct as he grew. I recall him vividly as the captain of games, as a most useful Prefect, enthusiastic in everything that came in his way, conscientious in his superintendence of meals in Hall, of Dormitory rules, of chapel processions; always taking the right line, as if by instinct, in matters of discipline, such as bullying and protection of the weak, and in matters of moral tone. He was a diligent learner, though not able to reach the highest rank in scholarship. Very early in life he conceived the desire to be a missionary, and his choice was for a cold climate."

In all this we see the child as "father of the man." There was plenty of fun and life in the school. "It was a healthy, free, active life we led," says one of the pupils. "I learned how to learn at S. Columba's College." The carman who drove the boys used to say, "I think the young gentlemen do leave their heart in the place." Yes, their hearts were with the old schoolroom, the chapel, the deer park, and the glen; and many a quaint anecdote is still told among the former alumni, such as the following of "Mr Bulmer's magpie'," from *Floreat Columba*, the college annual: "Of course many remember Mr Bulmer's magpie. One scene, in which the bird played an active part, comes back to me.

We were mustering at drill before the Warden's house, and Sergeant Gibson was brandishing his old umbrella and dressing up the ranks, while stragglers came down from the old schoolroom at a 'double.' Last of all came why not name him? Seymour Major, with the choicest of 'tuppenny' buns, brown, glistening and scorbutic with broken lump sugar a-top. It was a toothsome morsel, and, as he 'fell in,' he could not resist the temptation to sample its delights. Up went the Warden's window. 'Seymour, Seymour, what have you got there?' Seymour held forth his late purchase, and explained hardly necessary, indeed, for the object was large and easily seen 'A bun, sir.' 'Put it down at once, there, on the grass in front.' So Seymour stepped on the sacred spot, 'out of bounds,' as all know, and, to save his luncheon from the damp, put it on the projecting plinth under the common-room window and fell back into his place. Then the Warden's window closed and drill continued. 'First extension movement lock the thumbs, left in front one,' etc., etc. And still Seymour's bun simmered in the morning's sunlight. Tragedy, however, hovered near at hand. With a sudden flop and elevating of his tail, dropped Mr Bulmer's magpie before us on the grass, taking a quite disinterested glimpse at Seymour's bun. An awful fear fell on us Seymour had his name 'taken' twice for gross inattention could it be wondered at? Nearer and nearer came 'Mag,' and at last, with one light hop, reached the plinth, drove home his beak, and with an irritating 'keck, keck,' like the jarring laughter of an old man, sailed off with his prize to the heights of the Warden's beech.

"There is no moral, I regret to say. 'Mag' survived the theft and the bun for many years.

"But it was rough on Seymour, was it not?"

We find Henry Irwin's name in the College lists of athletes. "Those seem giant days to remember now," writes Mr Orpen, an old "boy" of S.C.C. "Then balls were always over the Marlay wall such tricks does memory play-and Henry Irwin kept fielders busy in the vicinity of the Fives Courts, to the weariness of the Bowler." It is said that one mighty ball from Irwin's bat almost struck the head of Mrs Parnell, mother of the redoubted Irish champion, Charles Stewart Parnell, and of Henry Tudor Parnell, a pupil at S. Columba's, of whom it is said that, "silent and imperturbable, he hated games, and was always working. He was a fine classic, and seemed to 'tumble' to Æschylus and Sophocles the first time he tried. Parnell's insight into dipus Rex was wonderful." The old Columbans knew how to work and how to play with zest and zeal, and we believe that these happy traditions remain.

CHAPTER II
AT KEBLE COLLEGE, OXFORD

THE next step in Henry Irwin's life was his matriculation at Keble College, in 1878. The deep enthusiasm felt for "Keble" in its early days exceeds, perhaps, anything that we in the colder light of the twentieth century can quite understand. The very name, reminding the students of the poetic leader who gave the impress of his tender imagination to the Oxford Revival, with the principle of "plain living and high thinking," which was the ideal of Keble College in its early days, gave to the place a charm, and added a certain *cachet* to every Keble man. As the present Head of the College (the Rev. Walter Lock, D.D.) has said: "To commemorate the holy memory of John Keble, and to carry on the work he had at heart, Keble College, Oxford, was founded in 1870. Its objects were twofold: (i) to answer to a widespread desire to make University education more accessible to the nation, and especially to those who were anxious to take Holy Orders in the Church of England, and (2) to insure that their education should be in the hands of Churchmen." Here, in an atmosphere corresponding to that which breathed in his own family circle, and which S. Columba's had fostered, Henry Irwin passed the happy years of his undergraduate life, bearing there much the same character as at school. Upright and clean in nature, full of spirits and goodwill, studious, but not attaining to a high rank in scholarship, he was every man's friend, and universally loved and trusted.

His College friend, the Rev. Percy Smythe, Vicar of Kettering, says: "When Irwin first went up to Keble, the College was just beginning to get over the reputation of being a new College in an old University. Some men still referred contemptuously to the College as *Kebble Hall*; and we used still to have sometimes cast at us a very insulting little rhyme which ran as follows:

"'There was a young freshman of Keble,
Whose legs were uncommonly feeble;
So he chartered a fly

To go down to the High,
A Sabbath-day's journey from Keble.'

"On the whole, however, the College held its own in the 'Varsity, and its reputation was increased in our day both by recently won triumphs on the river and by the popularity of Norman MacLachlan, captain of the University Cricket Eleven, who was a Keble man.

"The dons in those days were a remarkable set of men; the dear old Warden; then the Rev. Walter Lock (now Warden); Jayne, Illingworth, Herbert Gladstone, and others. The men did not strike me as remarkable. They were a level set, and there was an honest, straightforward, manly tone about the College; and though we seemed to ourselves an ordinary lot, there were men among us who were destined to make their mark: Winnington Ingram, now Bishop of London; Mike Rimington, of South African fame; Mackenzie, afterwards Principal of the Academy in Edinburgh; Wilson, afterwards Vicar of Portsea; and Douglas Eyre, so well known among workers in East London. Besides, there were dozens of men unknown to fame who are honestly serving God in their generation. Keble was just the school to turn out clean, hard-working Englishmen; what we might call a good level lot."

Henry Irwin kept up his reputation as an athlete; he rowed in the Torpids and Eights; played in his College Eleven and in the 'Varsity Fifteen. A letter of his, written at this time, may be of interest:

"KEBLE COLLEGE, Nov. 9, 1878.

"MY DEAR M. I have had a treat, to hear the two great preachers of Oxford, Dr Pusey and Canon Liddon: I only heard the former's sermon read by Mr Paget of Christ Church, as the doctors considered Pusey unfit to preach; of course it was a beautiful sermon, and Canon Liddon's of this afternoon was not less beautiful.

"We had a large number at Celebration this morning: I think there were about seventy. I wonder more don't avail themselves of the opportunity. You will be glad to hear that I am in the choir; or at least I am a probationer. Freshmen are only admitted as probationers. After the 'Varsity sermon, I and two others went off to High Celebration at SS. Philip and James; it was very nice indeed.

"It is curious to find men having exactly the same wishes as oneself; one of those who intend to go out as missionaries told me that his choice lay between South Africa and Newfoundland.

"That terrible ordeal 'Smalls' comes before Christmas; I believe it is not so bad as it is pictured, but I shall be very glad when it is over. I have bad luck, as the examination goes in alphabetical order, and they will begin this year from L, so I shall not have any chance of getting to S. Columba's College for the breaking up. Yours, H. I."

Another letter, simply headed "Saturday," but apparently written about the same time concerning a missionary meeting, shows the joyous interest taken in everything in his new life. Indeed, is anything equal to the joy of those young fellows who throw themselves into the best life of the University, life which may not always be intellectual, but is full of gladness and hope, to which steady work is a capital foil

"My DEAR M. I had a treat indeed last night, one I would not have missed for anything. The meeting took place in the Town Hall, and the room was full some time before the meeting began. The Bishop of Oxford was not there; he was ill. We opened with prayer, and then the Chairman introduced Mr Farler of the African Mission. He was splendid. He began his lecture from the time when he set out with Bishop Steere, for the first time, into the heart of Africa. He had very odd experiences on his journey, but arrived safely at the first town. Here he said he was very lonely when the Bishop left him, the only white man among a dense population of blacks. His first sermon was a great success, as the people came from all parts and were very eager to hear the new religion. He told us most amusing stories; one of them was, that knives and forks had never been seen before by the natives, and a large crowd gathered round every day at dinner to watch the white man eating; peals of laughter ran round as each piece was put into his mouth; it was incomprehensible why such trouble was taken when one had fingers ready made. Mr Farler told us that he found the greatest possible advantage in having a knowledge of medicine; and that he never would have got the influence he had obtained if he had not known how to cure the different diseases. The hardest part of doctoring was, that it took an immensity of time to find out what was wrong with the natives; for if you tapped them on the head, they would say *that* was the sore part; and then, if you touched the arm, *that* was the sore part, and so on."

Here we see the same deep interest in mission work that marked Henry Irwin as a boy; with the love of fun which so distinguished him later in his own missionary life, when hardships were relieved by his power of always seeing the humour of the situation.

Another letter, dated "Sunday," speaks of a sermon that Irwin had heard preached by Mr Richmond at S. Barnabas' Church, on the necessity of constant prayer, and advising his hearers to follow S. Paul's example, and remember in prayer those with whom they came in contact during their daily life, whether friends or not.

He now joined the Missionary Association of Keble College, to which the Warden gladly admitted him. He was asked to join the E.C.U., but replied plainly that he did not approve of joining any such societies (societies with a strong party bias) while a Freshman. For a similar reason he refused to hear Monsignor Capel, in spite of his reputation for eloquence.

More information we have not as to his College life. He speaks of playing football frequently, and how no one "who does not know what a delight it is to have every muscle strained to do its best, can appreciate this really grand game."

In the year 1881 Irwin took his degree, and left Oxford, having fully resolved on taking Holy Orders, with the ultimate aim of offering himself for the work of a missionary.

He was already known to his chums as "Pat," from his Irish origin and marked nationality, but it was not till he was in his first curacy that a colleague gave him the *sobriquet* of "Father Pat," which stuck to him ever after.

CHAPTER III
HIS FIRST CURACY RUGBY

ON leaving Oxford, where he took an ordinary Degree in 1881, Henry Irwin went for a time to Yarlet, as master in the Boys' School there, under the Rev. Walter Earle.

The following account of him is from the pen of Mr Earle himself, now resident at Bilton Grange, Rugby:

"Henry Irwin came to Yarlet, if I remember right, straight from the university, and remained about one and a half years.

"His ideas of the future had not then taken any very definite shape: his heart was always hot within him, and he threw the whole of that heart so much into the immediate present that it was absorbed in his life with the boys, their work, their play, their everything.

"Being a man of large sympathies, sunny, patient, untiring, earnest, loving, he was cut out for a most valuable schoolmaster; blessed with a vigorous healthy body and sunny nature, he always saw the better side of everybody's character; and if there was a worse, that worse would safely be confided to Pat Irwin, for a boy knew he was in good hands, and that his master only wanted to be trusted with the whole in order to be a real friend and helper.

"His life with me was naturally made up of (so called) little duties, but he was too thorough a man not to find a full sufficiency of greatness in the daily drudgery. Each day was ease, happy living, jolly comradeship: I cannot remember a grievance or rub; all was outspoken, nothing misunderstood, offence impossible.

"It was a cloudy sad time when he came to tell us that he had made up his mind to take Holy Orders and devote himself to parochial work; but his mind was a strong one, and what he meant, his resolution soon put into doing.

"Well do I remember saying to him (most reluctantly) when he came to acquaint me of his intention: 'You are right, you want a bigger field.'

"I felt he saw a larger future, and that his spirit had subtle powers and latent capabilities that ought to be free to choose what range they fancied.

"After he left me, he went to Rugby, during 1883. I used to hear of his busy life, his interest in the working men, the new Guild which he had started, his kindness to boys at the big school. He loved my "boys and would have them to tea at his rooms, and with that tea many a kind, wise, opportune bit of elder-brother advice would be thrown in.

"The last time I saw him was here at Bilton Grange on one of his short holidays: he arrived galloping down my drive on Lawrence's pony: I think I hear him shouting to me: 'Here's my war horse, dear old Lawrence's Taffy!' big sou'wester hat on the back of his head, face radiant with health and happiness, not much of the cleric in his attire that day! but a heart overflowing with goodwill to all men, and an irresistible manly influence which one felt must be the making of his missionary success: a kind of spirit-magnetism seemed to flow from the shake of his hand and the merry good-natured laugh.

"I can quite believe that he would wear himself out with work: he could not understand any half measures: 'all in all, or not at all,' was his motto.

"He came to Yarlet to teach boys, and the best teaching he ever gave was to us men: if there was any iron in us, 'Pat' was the iron to sharpen it: no one forgets him, there is no one who does not feel all the better for having known him, and we are assured that his blessed influence must still be circling forth, ever widening out, beyond the cognisance of his fellows, but never lost sight of by the great Omniscient Father."

Between the happy time at Yarlet and his first curacy, came the deepening spiritual experience of a Theological College. In 1882 Henry Irwin entered his name at Ely, and remained there for a year, when he was ordained Deacon. The Theological College at Ely was founded in 1876, by the generosity of Bishop Woodford, and has distinguished itself by sending forth priests, manly and hard-working, "into every diocese of England and Wales, into Scotland, Ireland, and far beyond into Australia, New Zealand, Africa, and India; into Canada and the West Indies." [See Canon Newbolt's Address at the Festival of Ely Theological College, June 4, 1901.]

In former days a man proceeded straight from the university to ordination, with the interim preparation only of reading for the Bishop's examination. He then at once took up work in school or parish, and it depended entirely on his Vicar or Rector whether he received any training for his sacred office that was worthy of the name. The wonder is that so many good clergymen were produced by such course; for the gap between lay and clerical life is too great to be bridged over merely by work and daily experience; it needs the calm of retirement, well-directed study, constant and mutual prayer. The spiritual life which has come into the Church of England's junior clergy dates chiefly from the foundation of the Theological Colleges, of which Cuddesdon and Ely may be said to stand first in regard to the number and character of the men emanating from them.

Belonging, as Henry Irwin did, to one of the Irish families which had been most earnest in the revival of Church life under such leaders as Beresford and Trench, he naturally took advantage of the privileges of theological and devotional training recently offered by the newly-founded college. He was respected and liked there, as at school and at the university; and in the "Report of Ely Theological College for 1902" he is referred to in terms of affectionate regret, his touching end being narrated.

Henry Irwin had the good fortune to find his first curacy under the Rev. John Murray, Rector of Rugby, than whom a more wise and ardent spirit never existed. His curates loved him as a father and a friend. Rugby is, in most people's minds, absorbed in the great public school, with the intense interest lent to it by the memory of Dr Arnold, who "trusted his boys," and the ever-fresh pages of "Tom Brown's School-days." But a fine town and noble churches exist there; and for two happy years Irwin acted as curate. He was ordained Priest in 1884, and then again the urgent call to mission work came to him, and (as will be seen) his Rector let him go with regret, but with approval of his choice.

We are indebted to Mr Irwin's former fellow-curate at Rugby, the Rev. T. H. Parker (now Vicar of Ettington, Stratford-on-Avon), for the following full and interesting account of the life there:

"Who among the clergy can deny a special affection for one's first curacy, if, at least, the conditions of life in it were reasonably favourable From the time that thoughts of ordination have occupied the mind of a young man, the place where he would begin his ministry for God, preach his first sermon, visit the sick and poor, and be regarded as holding a sacred office, looms large in his imagination. And when it is settled what and where this shall be, and a preliminary visit has been paid, there is an idealised view taken of Rector and fellow-curates, of Church and district, of the rooms that will be at once a base of operations and a refuge from publicity. I do not know that Irwin, when it was arranged that the Rector of Rugby was to give him a title for ordination, could have easily put his feelings into words, or would have put them into just such words as these. But Trinity Sunday, 1883, was a great day to him, for it brought to an end his year of special training for Holy Orders at Ely Theological College, and launched him on the course to which he had long looked forward, a course of parochial work for two years in some well-ordered parish at home and then pioneer work in mission fields abroad.

"It was the friendly commendation of the Rev. Hedley Vicars, who had been with Irwin at Keble, that brought him to the knowledge of the Rev. John Murray, Rector of Rugby, with the result that he became one of the four assistant curates. The others were, at that time, the Revs. F. Northcote Smith, Hedley Vicars, and A. O. Tisdall; but in September, 1883, the Rev. F. Northcote Smith left, and at

Christmas the vacancy was filled by the ordination and arrival of Henry Tudway Coney, who had been with Irwin at Ely. The curates now certainly formed a happy family: three of them were Irishmen and three were Ely men, and they were further knit together in the bonds of friendship and by thorough keenness and pretty good capacity. The Rector, moreover, was proud of his curates, and put great trust in them, and the parish was thoroughly well worked.

"It was at that time fairly workable. The population did not exceed 9000, so none of the clergy had more than 2000 people to look after, and their districts were compact. As to churches, besides the Parish Church, which is admitted to be one of Butterfield's most successful restorations, and which holds about 900 people, there was Holy Trinity Church, technically a chapel-of-ease, but itself larger and finer than most Parish Churches. This was built from designs by Sir George Gilbert Scott, since whose death it has been considerably improved by Mr Bodley, and it holds at least 700 people. And the services were as follows: Daily Matins in the Parish Church at 7.30, and daily Evensong in Holy Trinity at 5.30: Holy Communion on Sundays was at 7 and at 9 in the Parish Church, and on the first Sunday in the month at n, while it was celebrated in Holy Trinity Church every Sunday at 8 and on the third Sunday in the month at n. On Holy Days and on Thursdays there were also celebrations, and sometimes for the sick and aged, for some society or guild, or upon special occasions. So every week each priest on the staff celebrated at least once, and in the matter of preaching, if any preached more than once it was the Rector or the senior curate, and not one of the juniors. The schools in the parish were Church Schools, and the clergy gave religious instruction in them on two mornings in the week, and superintended the teaching on Sundays, and there were several classes and guilds. So there was plenty of work, but not too much. All was carefully arranged at a convocation held at the Rectory, week by week, on Monday mornings, the rule being that nobody outside it was to know when or where anyone was going to preach, and that each member of the staff, when it was settled what he had to do, was held responsible for it, and for doing it punctually and efficiently.

"Irwin, therefore, was kept busy during his time at Rugby, and had variety of work, but was not overweighted. In visiting, which was held to be of great importance, he spent two or three hours every afternoon, and he put a good deal of affection and zeal into his district. Through the middle of this ran, like a crooked thread, Gas Street and Finder's Lane, where some of the poorest people in the town lived and some of the most unruly. Two public houses kept guard at the top of Gas Street, and at the further end another public house and a lodging house kept watch and ward. The place was honeycombed with courts and alleys, with the usual result that quarrels were frequent and fights periodical.

"Here, one night early in his career, Irwin came upon a man fighting with his wife. Without a moment's hesitation he ran in to part them. And when the man's wrath was turned upon himself 'Look here,' he said, and he promptly pulled off his coat,'if you want to fight anyone, you can fight me.' The affair was over, and Irwin went to his rooms slightly heated. He had done an unconventional thing; perhaps the old Adam was still strong in his blood, for, truth to say, he had enjoyed himself well.

"None the less, it would be quite a mistake to imagine incidents like this came often in Irwin's life at Rugby, or that he was in those days the mission-priest who made himself one with the people in all conditions of life. His photograph gives a different impression, and a truer one. He was, during the first two years of his clerical life, the well-trained young ecclesiastic, brought, and not unwillingly, to sustain his part in a well-ordered and established system, being run, some would say, into ecclesiastical grooves. He was earnest and dutiful, but he was diffident. Full of fun and high spirits with his fellow-curates when work was done, but finding some things far from easy; worrying himself a good deal about his sermons, practising a little elocution, and anxious to overcome a difficulty he found in pronouncing 'negligences and ignorances' when called upon to say the Litany. He was not yet what he became later, his personality was not developed. He was too fresh from the mould to run free, and it may well be that the time had not come for freedom.

At any rate Irwin owned then, and afterwards, that he owed a great debt to Ely and to the dominant influences of his first curacy.

"Personally he soon became popular at Rugby, but was always thoroughly humble, which was doubtless one reason for his popularity. It was not long before he was on good terms with most of the men and boys with whom he came in contact.

"Perhaps he was least at ease in a lady's drawing-room, where he had a tendency to get hot, and to long for the open air. That, it must be confessed, was really his element: his nature was akin to it. And when, in 1884, the definite offer of mission-work in British Columbia came to him, this may have had its influence in making him eager at once to go. His Rector knew from the beginning that after two years' work at Rugby, Irwin's intention was to go abroad; that was, so to speak, in the bond; and if he expected to have more than two years rather than less of Irwin's help, he could not find it in his heart to resist the generous impulse of his curate.

"I find from the Parish Magazine that Irwin went with the workhouse inmates on an excursion to Coombe Abbey within a month of his coming to Rugby, and again with St Andrew's Guild to the same place a few weeks later. To expeditions of this sort he was in himself almost a pledge of success. Misfortunes, if they occurred, had the same effect upon him that they had on Mark Tapley: his good spirits could always be relied upon to relieve the tedium of a journey, and his good nature to bring out the shy or the neglected. The guild in those days was strong, and, under the care of the Rev. Hedley Vicars, had come to number nearly a hundred men and boys. Their cricket eleven was strong also, but found in Irwin a useful as well as an agreeable member. He was a lively bat, with the capacity to bring off a big hit or two, and in all departments of the game he was a most unselfish player. At football he was even better than at cricket, and the Rugby Town fifteen, hearing of the arrival of a curate who was an Oxford 'blue' speedily offered him a place in their team, which thought no small things of itself. He played occasionally, and did them good service; but one Saturday afternoon he returned home with an unmistakable black eye. Tisdall, with whom he lived at that time, made a great effort with a box of paints and his utmost skill to lay on a coat of flesh-colour; but his patient laughed so outrageously during the operation that the result was not very satisfactory. At any rate the Rector on the following day saw beneath the surface, and laid an interdict on a Sunday preacher engaging in football on a Saturday afternoon.

"When Irwin first went to Rugby, he lodged at 112 Railway Terrace; but before long he and Tisdall joined forces, and took a small house in Bath Street, which in those days looked over the glebe allotment gardens, and so was named Glebeview. Mr and Mrs Masters kept house for them, and here they were thoroughly comfortable and happy. They were able also to exercise a little their hospitable spirits. Irwin had two cousins named Wilson at Rugby School who sometimes came to tea, and brought a posse of companions. And late in the evenings there would often drop in a friend or two of their own age and standing, schoolmasters perhaps whose work was done for the day, to have a sociable chat and smoke a quiet pipe. There were other visitors too; sometimes from a distance, but much more often from close at home, who rang the bell and wanted 'to see Mr Irwin, if you please, and could he let Mrs B have a grocery ticket' The Rector made it a general rule that relief tickets were only to be given by the district-visitors, holding that it spoiled a curate's pastoral visitation if he was thought to have them about his person. But somehow tickets were often obtained by these applicants, or something which they liked still better.

"I suppose that Irwin, at all times in his life, was willing to give almost anything he had to almost anyone who wanted it. He was no great accumulator of goods, and even what came as a gift often went as a gift, and made with him but a temporary sojourn. When he was about to leave Rugby, at Easter 1885, many people wished to give him parting presents, and he accepted a few books, a mariner's compass from the men's Bible Class which used to meet in his room at Glebeview, and a case of sacred vessels for the communion of the sick, subscribed for by the congregations: but when he could do it without hurting their kindly feelings, he pleasantly urged his friends not to load up a missionary with baggage.

"In the *Parish Magazine* for April 1885 the following valedictory note appeared: 'The general regret which is felt at the approaching departure of the Rev. H. Irwin to labour in the distant diocese of New Westminster found expression in a very interesting gathering, at the Coffee Tavern, on Thursday, March 26, the choirs of both churches having invited him to meet them that they might have the pleasure of spending a last evening with him, and of telling him how highly they held him in regard, and how heartily they bade him God-speed in his new work.

"'Mr Irwin's brother clergy were kindly included in the invitation, and a goodly number sat down to a substantial tea. The Rector spoke with much affection and gratitude of the help and comfort Mr Irwin had been to him and his flock, of the brightness he had shed around him, and the simplicity and earnestness with which he had fulfilled his duties; and hoped that some day he would recross the Rocky Mountains and visit Rugby again, where he would always find warm hearts that still remembered and loved him.

"'Messrs W. H. Linnell and G. E. Over for the Parish Church, and Messrs Miller and Orchard for Holy Trinity Church choir, gave utterance in turn to the sincere regret with which all would bid farewell to Mr Irwin, and the deep interest they must ever feel in his future happiness and success. They then begged his acceptance of two beautifully bound books, viz.: "The Imitation of Christ" and "The Christian Year."

"'Mr Irwin, with his wonted cordiality, thanked his friends for their kind words and gifts, and said that it was no new impulse that was severing the tie which had bound them together so happily, but a resolution formed years ago, before he came to Rugby, when he had felt moved to devote himself to the work of a missionary.

"'It goes without saying that such an assembly was nothing if not musical, and the songs most appropriately ended with "Auld Lang Syne."'

"The following month the Rector added these words: 'Many will feel interested to hear that our good friend the Rev. H. Irwin left Liverpool on the 1st of May by steamer for New York, whence he will proceed across North America to the scene of his future labours on the western coast of that Continent. Numerous were the tokens of regard offered to him ere his departure, but chiefest of all was a compact and handsome travelling case, containing the sacred vessels and other articles necessary for the administration of the Holy Communion.

"'In his far-off home this useful and fitting memorial of their affection will often recall to his thoughts the friends he has left behind him.'"

It has not been found possible to procure many of Irwin's letters written to Rugby friends, but the following extracts appeared in the *Parish Magazine*. Writing on September 10, 1885, he says: "I received from Mr Lawrence yesterday the beautifully illuminated list of my friends in Rugby (who had given him the Holy Communion vessels), whom I need not say I remember every time I have to make use of their gift. It seems as if we were all together again now, as I read their names over, and I wish that you would kindly let them know that away here in the wild West such a memory is a wonderful help."

And again a year later, "The year and a half I have been here I have had fairly hard but the pleasantest of work. Most of the time I have been in the saddle. Our district is so large, and the population so small and scattered, that there's nothing for it but galloping from Sunday to Sunday, and often on Sunday itself we have fairly long rides between services. ... I cannot tell you how miserable it is meeting men from the mines who have lost their all, tramping over the country with their blankets on their backs, and not a cent in their pockets, getting a meal here and there for love, and trying to obtain work." But there were some, he went on to say, who were only too willing to help themselves to other people's property, and he concluded the letter with the account of an adventure by which a member of his congregation had nearly lost his life at the hands of two ruffianly "highwaymen."

In a letter of about the same date, referring to some Prayer-books which had been sent to him, he wrote: "You cannot think how much they are valued away here in the west. We have so many from the old country who feel better at even the sight of a Prayer-book. ... I am just now hard at work getting a church built here in Donald, a little railway town of 600 men, and if you know any people who would like to give us help towards furnishing it, I should be thankful for the smallest trifle."

In response to this appeal, the Rugby members of the All Saint's Guild, a branch of which was formed at Rugby before Irwin left for New Westminster, sent a brass cross for the altar of S. Peter's Church at Donald, and a silk veil and some linen for use at celebrations of Holy Communion. They also gave a certain amount for some years to the diocesan funds, sending it to the Rev. H. H. Mogg, [Secretary of the Missionary Association for New Westminster] and £20 was once sent to Irwin direct, probably to help him to get materials for building at Donald, where he laid his own hands vigorously both to the axe and the workman's hammer.

Lastly, there is an interesting and amusing letter written to Mr Masters concerning his clothes, and dated "Kamloops, August 10, 1887." It runs: "Thank you for the clothes, which arrived safely and are a great blessing to me. You cannot think how nice it is to feel respectable out here., where one has to put on, and up with, almost anything in the way of coats. There is no great symmetry, as you know, in ready-made clothes, and when a parson has only the rainbow colours to choose from it is hard to be quite sombre, and certainly there's little in the ready-made clothes here of the dim religious light. You would hardly know me in many of my costumes. Last trip I started with those riding pants you sent me, but after about 300 miles they went to pieces, and I had to get into a vile kind of garment they call overalls, striped like the zebra, and cut like a sailor's pantaloons. You would open your eyes wide to see a parson at work out here. . . . The hot weather still continues, and it is hot, and no mistake; up to 101 in the shade. But after a certain amount of broiling one's skin gets quite hardened. I am now as hard as a cake and a browned one at that. You can guess that one has a benefit when you have to ride from early morning till the evening under a sun like ours, and that for perhaps a month at a stretch. I finished in June a trip of 570 miles in the saddle, and by the end of that time I was a dirty brown, very like an Indian. . . . I think that the longer I live here the more I wonder why people leave quiet peaceful homes in the old country to rough it in Colonial life. There is absolutely no comfort here for the first five years, and a man must have quite a small fortune with him to give him a good enough start to make a home in that short time. You may be surprised at this, but it has been the experience of many who had all the best of the country to choose from in early days, and have had more advantages than any later comers are likely to get. I am looking forward to having a visit home about Christmas, but I cannot say yet whether I shall get off. Of course, if I do, I shall come to see you all at Rugby, and it will be a greater pleasure for me to see you than you me."

Bishop Sillitoe paid a visit to Rugby in August 1887, and preached in the Parish Church; but Irwin did not come until 1889 when he stayed a few days, and addressed a meeting in the parochial schools. He came again in 1894, and joined the clerical staff again for a month or so while the Rector was away for his holiday. He was a different man then in many ways from the curate of ten years before, but in spirit he was the same, and a kind and cheery spirit Rugby always found it.

The Rev. C. J. Whitehead, of South Newington Vicarage, Banbury, gives the following account of his friendship with Henry Irwin:

"I knew and liked dear Pat Irwin very much; but my intimacy with him was only too brief. I went to Rugby as an assistant master in Hillbrow Preparatory School in January, 1883; and that same year Irwin came to Rugby as curate. During the few years he was there, we made friends, and he was kind enough to invite me to stay with his father in Ireland. I was still at Rugby when he came back from his first term of work as a missionary in British Columbia, where he had already done noble work, especially at Kamloops. The Canadian Pacific Railway was then being constructed, and Pat's work with the very cosmopolitan set of men at work at Kamloops, the head-quarters of that section of the line, was very remarkable.

"He brought with him on that occasion, a number of photographs, which he showed to the boys in the school and to the masters; and we had long talks till late at night, when he recounted his adventures to us; such as, riding 500 miles on one horse in a week; recovering his horse which had been stolen by Indians; avoiding an Indian murderer in a vast forest. His influence over the 'very rough diamonds' he had to deal with was wonderful; he got them to build churches, and (better still) to attend them, and he pulled many a poor fellow who had gone utterly wrong, straight again.

"That visit to Rugby was the last I saw of him. He went back to Ireland for a little time when his good father died, and I think he held the living; but his love for British Columbia was too strong, and he returned there. I remember a friend of mine who had been round the world and had met Pat in British Columbia, telling me that he was the most remarkable man he had come across."

Yes, truly, a remarkable man was Henry Irwin; not for intellectual gifts so much as for character. He was the friend of every man. To him every human soul was of intense value: he tried to look on men as the angels do, "with larger, other eyes than ours"; and in this he is an example of the true Socialism the only sort that will ever work the socialism which bids a man give his life for others.

CHAPTER IV
IN KAMLOOPS, BRITISH COLUMBIA

AT last, in 1885, the day came when Henry Irwin's dream was to be fulfilled, and having got his training under so good a master as Mr Murray of Rugby, he was to go forth to test his mettle on a wider field.

As a boy, Irwin had laughingly declared his intention of choosing a cold climate and being a missionary there; and he now fulfilled this intention by choosing British Columbia as the province, and New Westminster the diocese, where he would begin work. Although he had always declared his intention of doing missionary work, yet in British Columbia he never (or very rarely) worked among the native population; he rather turned to the Colonists, among whom, indeed, such ardent workers are greatly needed.

The history of the Church in British Columbia which (in 1909) is celebrating its Jubilee may be shortly set forth by a quotation from a leaflet issued by the Association for New Westminster.

"THE DIOCESE OF NEW WESTMINSTER AND KOOTENAY

"New Westminster is a third of the vast Diocese of British Columbia, divided for purposes of organization, and in 1900 again sub-divided into New Westminster and Kootenay. As yet the two halves are under one Bishop, but the way is prepared for a new See when funds are raised.

"This diocese, as large as France, lies between the Rocky Mountains and the Pacific. The great Fraser River flows through it. It is 40,000 square miles larger than the United Kingdom.

"There are some 100,000 of population, consisting of

"(a) English immigrants. These are the main part of the population; and mainly of the wage-earning classes; therefore the Church in

British Columbia is not yet able to be self-supporting like the Church in Eastern Canada. The call to help our own Colonists is strong; if England does not care for the souls of her own children, who is to do so (Gal. vi. 10.)

"(b) Indians. There are some 11,000 Indians in the diocese. These, the original possessors of the land, claim our care as an act of justice. Many are Christians, and 1,500 are under the special care of the Ven. Archdeacon of Yale: 250 are Communicants of the Church of England. An excellent school under Sisters of the English Church, at Yale, receives Indian girls in one department, and Colonists' daughters in another. A school for Indian boys (urgently needed) has also been established: The New England Company have taken this in hand.

"(c) Chinese. Of these there are about 9000 working, chiefly as servants, laundry men, and market gardeners. They come as heathen; shall they go away without instruction in the Christian religion Does not the martyr blood, shed by native Christians in China, cry aloud for spiritual help for these people when working for Christians in a Christian land A Chinese Mission, opened in 1891, has lately been successful; but the Bishop appeals for more help. *The Industries of this Busy Corner of our Empire* are salmon canning, coal mining, gold digging, and fruit growing. All these contribute to the comfort or luxury of English people. Let us return a gift of goodwill to the workers.

"History of the Diocese

"British Columbia in 1858 passed from the hands of the Hudson Bay Company to the position of a Crown Colony, and is now an integral confederated province of the Canadian Dominion. In 1859, the Diocese of Columbia was founded under Bishop Hills, and endowed by the Baroness Burdett Coutts. It was found to be too large a diocese to be workable, and at last was sub-divided into three: Columbia, Caledonia, and New Westminster.

"The latter was founded, in 1879, by Bishop Hills. Bishop Acton Windeyer Sillitoe, the first Bishop, who worked with the most earnest zeal, died in 1894. Bishop John Dart succeeded in 1895, and, in spite of financial difficulties which had supervened in Diocesan funds, great progress has been made in the work of the Church."

What led Henry Irwin to select this special field for his labours, we do not exactly know, though it is said to have been suggested to him by a sermon which he heard. We may be sure that the choice was made with thought and prayer, and that the Holy Spirit led him to this sphere of work.

After correspondence with the Bishop, Acton Windeyer Sillitoe, it was decided that Mr Irwin should begin work in Kamloops on the C.P.R. or Canadian Pacific Railway, as assistant to Mr Horlock, the Vicar, and thither he proceeded in 1885.

The town of Kamloops lies on the South Thompson River, which, after making a bend at an acute angle, runs straight for many miles under a line of hills of which the most prominent is known as Mount Paul. To the south spreads a beautiful prospect of hill and plain, but westward run the river and the railway through a panorama as strange as a mirage or an optical delusion. It consists of a series of miniature hills and valleys of sand, extending for miles along the north side of the river; doubtless the deposit of a far wider prehistoric stream. Barren and weird and strange look these quaint little hills, some thirty to forty feet high, with crenelated summits and a few stunted fir trees here and there; with cave and creek and winding valleys, they resemble the abode of gnomes or pigmies.

The C.P.R. runs through the main street of Kamloops. When Henry Irwin arrived there, no church had yet been built. Service was held in the court-house. The inhabitants largely consisted of the men employed on the C.P.R., then in progress of formation.

These men were of mixed nationalities, many of them wild and rough. The bright young Irishman, full of zeal and enthusiasm, threw himself heartily into the new life.

The exquisite air of British Columbia, light, bracing and health-giving, was congenial to him and spurred him on to new energy. He quickly became a favourite, his work extending far and wide, for he was really an itinerant parson, assisting Mr Horlock, the Vicar of Kamloops, by riding into the mountains to the mining camps and elsewhere. Few and far between were the clergy in British Columbia at that date.

The name "Father Pat" appears to have at once been given to Henry Irwin, and to have been constantly used for him by the rougher portion of his flock. It suited his nature, which combined with a devout and earnest spirit a natural winning humour.

A friend who knew him in Oxford and at Rugby says: "he was always the same straightforward, simple, fearless, true-hearted character; and it was this simplicity and utter fearlessness that gave him the power which he possessed, especially among men of the roughest class, and made him attractive to a very large circle of friends. I gave him the name of Pat in those first days at Oxford, the name which stuck to him all his life, and was used by everyone who knew him, in the new world as well as in the old." [The Rev. Hedley Vicars, of All Saints' Rectory, Huntingdon.]

A characteristic anecdote is told that shows his pluck and spirit, qualities sure to win him friends among the rough but hearty "boys" of the Far West. It was regarded by them as a good joke to make a fool of a parson, or a padre, as he is generally called out West. Therefore seeing a bright, well-dressed young fellow as Irwin then was, they at once concluded he was a milksop, and soon asked, "Can you ride?"

"I was bred in the saddle," he answered.

"Then you won't mind trying this nag, though he's a bit spirited"

"All the better for that."

And Irwin mounted a fine-looking creature, which however, was that nasty thing a buck-jumper.

Now of all uncomfortable animals, your buck-jumper, as described to me, is the worst.

His mind seems sets on no other thing than to break his rider's bones and shatter his nerves. Gathering up his four legs and humping up his back, he executes a *pas seul* unequalled for its power of unseating a rider. Up he goes in the air, and alighting on all four feet with a thud that makes a man feel as if all his teeth had been suddenly extracted, he then executes a few caracoles with his hind feet above the level of the rider's head; and if that unfortunate be still in the saddle, the beast resumes the agreeable exercise.

Harry Irwin had learned in his Irish home to ride any ordinary horse with ease, even bare-backed. But a buck-jumper was a new experience. He soon found out the trick that had been played on him, but kept his temper and his nerve; and though thrown and shaken, he remounted once and again, hating to be beaten, and would have done so a third time but that his friends interposed, assuring him he had given ample proof of pluck; in which even his tormentors concurred. They never called him "milksop" again.

CHAPTER V
AMONG THE SELKIRKS

IT was while he was at Kamloops that Mr Irwin met the sweet lady who was the love of his life, and whose influence worked so strongly in him after her passing from this world.

Miss Frances Stuart Innes was the youngest daughter of a gentleman who held a public appointment in Victoria, British Columbia. Her elder sister had married the Rev. A. Shildrick, now and for many years past Rector of Holy Trinity Cathedral Church, New Westminster. At the time when Mr Irwin went out to British Columbia, Mr Shildrick was senior assistant priest in Kamloops district, and settled in the Spallumcheen Valley, the district where Enderby and Vernon lie. He rode to and fro on his missionary work (as we have seen from his letter in the last chapter Mr Irwin also did), holding services "from house to house," in scattered ranches. The people he ministered to, though seldom of gentle breeding, were almost invariably hospitable and welcoming to the clergy, and in some cases very appreciative of their ministrations.

Frances Innes was one of those gentle, timid creatures who appeal most powerfully to a brave man's heart by their essential womanliness. Spiritually minded, of strong religious principle, she was yet so shy that it was hard to persuade her to go into the world alone, even for necessary business. She must have been very charming in appearance, though not regularly beautiful, Soft curling brown hair, blue eyes very expressive, and a sweet childlike smile. Merry and bright at home, the life of the family, there yet was a pathos in her look which seems natural now to us who know how soon that lovable personality was to be removed from this world.

Henry Irwin was one to whom such womanly charm especially appealed; and when Frances Innes, on her way to spend a long visit with her sister Mrs Shildrick, stopped first for a time at the house of Mr and Mrs Horlock of Kamloops (old friends of her family), it was natural that the young assistant priest should be drawn to her irresistibly. When she left Kamloops for the Spallumcheen Valley, he soon found his way thither; and the end was a happy engagement, a complete and perfect union of hearts, which lasted four years before their marriage could be arranged. No love letters remain, or none are permitted for use here. It is felt that the departed would have wished to shield their most sacred feelings from the world's eyes. "Not easily forgiven are they who lay bare the marriage chambers of the heart." [Emerson.]

In the year 1887, Mr Irwin's sphere of work was moved to Donald, a busy centre of the C.P.R., lying close upon the Rocky Mountains, between these and the Selkirks. A glance at the map will show that whereas Kamloops is in a district of comparatively low hills diversifying the plain, Donald is among all the glories of the mountains. The Rockies are well named: Stony Mountains they were called by the early settlers, and stony indeed they are. The snow which lies upon them does not cover their nakedness with its downy softness all the year round as in the Swiss mountains, but the bare ribs of the giants stand out in summer, gaunt and terrible. To a traveller on the C.P.R. after days on the level prairie, which becomes monotonous despite its lovely varied greens stretching away into a sea-like distance, it is refreshing at Calgary to observe the delicate outline of the Rockies, softened by haze and distance. Forty-three peaks can be counted from one point in Calgary. Thenceforth to the traveller all is one succession of beauty. The upward strain and climb of the panting engine leads through a range of foothills, broken by picturesque glades and gullies; and then at last the Rockies begin to assert themselves with their strange and weird forms. The words of Scott exaggerated as regards the Trossachs of which he wrote are literally true of these passes of the West:?

"Not a setting beam could glow
Within the dark ravines below,
Where twined the path in shadow hid
Round many a rocky pyramid,
Shooting abruptly from the dell
Its thunder-splintered pinnacle;
Round many an insulated mass,

> The native bulwarks of the pass,
> Huge as the tower which builders vain
> Presumptuous reared on Shinar's plain.
> The rocky summits, split and rent,
> Formed turret, dome, or battlement,
> Or seemed fantastically set
> With cupola or minaret."

I have seen a mountain on which appeared to be the ruins of a feudal castle; not only with its towers and bastion, but also with a Gothic doorway approached by broken steps, and a natural bridge cast across the ravine, all from the unaided hand of Nature. Then the traveller tarries on his way to visit the "Lakes in the Clouds," approached from Laggan, where Indian ponies await the tourist. There are three of these lakes, each of its own special hue, lapis lazuli blue, emerald green and the exquisite blue of the peacock. Glaciers, too, lie between the peaks, one (at the spot named "Glacier") is said to be vast enough to contain within itself all the icefields of Switzerland; and there are smaller ones here and there which repay a visit. Beside one of these recently dwelt an old man bearing the name of Hathaway, and claiming descent from the kin of Shakspere's wife, strange link between the old world and the new.

Arrived at the summit, the traveller begins his descent through the majestic scenery of the Kicking-Horse Pass. [Various reasons are given for this strange name; it may be a rude word-picture of the tearing, plunging torrent at the bottom of the pass.] Its jagged summits climbing the sky, pines darkly clothing the lower rocks, and leading the eye down, down, down to an abyss where the Kicking-Horse River gleams white and foaming below. In the gathering gloom of a summer night we saw it, a young moon rising behind the peaks and glinting on little lakes and tracts of snow among them. The Canadian Pacific train winds its slow and cautious route by curve and precipice, and for all the dreadful gradients, accidents very seldom occur.

It was in 1887, when the C.P.R. was diligently and swiftly laying its line from the Rockies to the Pacific, that Donald was a centre of great activity. Now it is a dead town. Hardly an inhabited house remains. The church erected by Father Pat has been removed; the vicarage is at Golden; every good house has been taken elsewhere, as is so easily done with the wooden buildings of the West. [When it was desired to move the Church of S. Paul's, Vancouver, it was done by means of a windlass worked by one old pony!] Nothing is more sad and strange than these new ruins of the Far West. Without the dignity of age, without mystery or beauty, the shattered relics of the wooden shacks and gimcrack stores stare from their empty window-holes, and lean in ghastly fashion, ready to fall with the next tempest, while all the ground is strewn with their debris.

Nor is one of these towns more gracious in its rapid growth. All is for speed and immediate use; the question of beauty does not enter the builder's mind; the only sign of a desire to save appearances being the large square sham fronts of the stores. But the spot in which Donald stands, close under the Selkirks and beside the Columbia River, is very fine; the air is delicious, and the absolute freedom from all social conventionality is attractive to many.

The making of the line was accompanied by many dangers, one of the chief arising from the frequent snow-slides. In the summer months, when snows begin to melt, vast masses of the liberated snow will descend and bury hut or man beneath it. In one of these accidents, at Donald, Father Pat first showed the characteristics which later made his name proverbial, and himself beloved among the rough settlers of British Columbia. In the first year when the C.P.R. ran straight through to the coast (1887), when about half the great snowsheds that now protect the railway had been built, but much of the line still lay exposed, such an accident occurred. A report came to Donald that part of the line was blocked by a snow-slide. The snow-plough was sent out to clear the way, and while this was being done, a second slide occurred in which Mr Green, the conductor of the snow-plough, was killed. As soon as this sad news was made known, the superintendent and other men went out to the summit of the pass to clear the road and to see what could be done. The snow was still coming down in small slides, the way was blocked, and Donald was cut off from communication with these men. Mrs Green was wild with anxiety, and her husband's body could not be brought in, as the line was blocked by masses of snow. "Father Pat" resolved if possible to relieve the poor widow's anxiety and restore to her the remains of her beloved husband. He took a toboggan or handsleigh, which could move over the snow where an engine could not cut its way through; and disregarding the danger threatening at every step from the snow-slides still going on, he made his way to where the dead man lay, took the body, reverently covered, on the little sleigh, and brought it in to Donald. He was away two days and a night. While under the protection of a snowshed, he would watch and wait for an opportunity to pass in safety to the next. He spent that night alone with the dead man on the desolate and dangerous road.

During the same event, another wife was terribly anxious for her husband, who was among those who were cut off by the snow from communication with his home at Donald. Half mad with fear for her husband's safety, the poor woman came to Father Pat for news. "I have heard from your husband," said Mr Irwin. "He is all right, and will soon be home." It was true that the man was safe, and he was ere long restored to his wife. But it was not the fact that Father Pat had heard from him. He afterwards confessed this to the wife whose mind he had calmed and relieved, dare we say, by his splendid lie "I did it," said he, "lest I should have you distracted on my hands."

It was Irwin's characteristic, that he acted boldly on impulse, led by his heart as often as by his head, perhaps oftener. And this loving impulsiveness won him the hearts of the people. [I am indebted for these anecdotes to Miss Nelson of Kaslo, B.C.]

When in Donald, Mr Irwin boarded with a Mrs Lovelock; she had another boarder, named Black, who took an active interest in Church work in Donald. He was the best helper that Father Pat had there in that respect; perhaps the only one to render much service. There was no church at Donald when Mr Irwin went there; services were held (as usual in such cases) in the Court-House. He had a little organ which he played himself, and moved from place to place for services, on a trolly on the line. At first only women attended these services.

Religion seems to form but a small part of the life of male colonists, even of those who have been accustomed to fulfil its duties in the home country. Nor was Father Pat a brilliant or specially attractive preacher. Sound Church doctrine, clothed in simple language, was what he gave his flock, as one can judge from the specimens of his sermons remaining to us. His view was that of the old Tractarians: "Worship the Deity according to the rites He has prescribed through His Church, and lean not on the gifts of men." Once when a hearer praised him for a good sermon that he had given, his face fell; a look of sadness and even of reproach stole over it, and he said, turning away: "We go to church to worship God."

But as his hand was ever at the service of others, so they became willing and glad to help him in things practical, and he soon had a little church erected in Donald. These tiny wooden churches do not take long to build. A clearing in the primeval forest, a few boards, much energy on the part of the priest, some kindly help given by others, and a place of worship may be erected at the cost of £100 or even less.

When the church at Donald was completed, Mr Irwin remembered his former parish at Kamloops and its needs. He collected on several occasions among his new flock money for a church at Kamloops. Records of the sums he sent for that purpose still remain in the minutes of the church, as also a list of the many places where Father Pat went in a wide circuit to hold divine service in the wilds. It would seem as if he were ubiquitous. One can hardly conceive of a priest ministering in so many spots within so short a space of time, many of them being so far distant and inaccessible. But "where there's a will there's a way," and his almost abnormal activity now revealed itself.

The Rev. C. F. Yates, Rector of Golden, British Columbia, gives us details of some of these mission tours. He says: "Father Pat did not confine his work to the main line of the C.P.R. but journeyed down the Arrow Lakes, services being held as far south as Nelson, then a mere mining camp. We find, too, that he followed the Columbia from Golden to the Kootenay River, services being recorded at these places. Some six or eight clergy now occupy the territory thus covered, divided into five or six parishes."

Kamloops Church was built while Mr Shildrick was in England, and the Rev. Canon Cooper was appointed Vicar of Kamloops for a time, Mr Shildrick returning to it from England. Mr Horlock had also gone to England for a year's rest and change.

It will be well here to quote a passage from the memoir of Bishop Sillitoe, showing the state of Church work in these parts. ["Church Work in British Columbia," by Herbert H. Gowen (Longmans).]

The Bishop and Mrs Sillitoe had been to England, where the annual meeting of the New Westminister mission was held, in London, the Marquis of Lome speaking at it. They had been present at "the ever-memorable Jubilee Service in Westminster Abbey, at which the whole Empire lifted up its heart to God for Queen Victoria's glorious and happy reign."

Now, on his return to his diocese (1887) the Bishop was warmly welcomed by his people.

"At Donald, an address, signed by some forty persons, was presented at the C.P.R. station, in the darkness of a stormy night, to greet the Bishop. The next day being Sunday, the Bishop recommenced diocesan work by celebrating the Holy Communion, and preaching morning and evening to crowded congregations, in the new church, fitly called S. Peter's the first church in the Rocky Mountains.

"At Kamloops, the visit was marked by a Confirmation on the Monday, and a conference with the clergy on the Wednesday. A parish *conversazione* was also held, and an address of welcome presented on behalf of the citizens of Kamloops.

"The more official welcome was given in the city of New Westminster, where a large number of friends, including the Executive Committee of the Diocese, met the Bishop and Mrs Sillitoe on October 17. An address was presented, and what was more, the affectionate greetings of all emphasized the gladness of heart with which the inhabitants of New Westminster again saw their Bishop and his wife.

"The year was marked by one other circumstance deserving of notice.

"On the Festival of S. Andrew an interesting event took place in the Church of the Holy Trinity, New Westminster, when a beautiful pastoral staff was presented to the Bishop in the name of the clergy and communicants of the diocese, as a token of personal love and esteem."

Bishop Sillitoe and his wife were deservedly beloved, for they endeavoured to draw forth the best that was in all around them; and many a visit did they pay to spots even more inaccessible then than now, confronting dangers and hardships, to visit the Indians and settlers in the wilder parts. Mrs Sillitoe's letters quoted in "Church Work in British Columbia," and the diary of the Bishop, set these forth in picturesque words.

Father Pat's work lay to some extent among the Indians. A few of his missionary excursions led him to their settlements, but not much record is left of his special intercourse with them. He did not know the language and had to rely on an interpreter. His friend Mrs Macartney relates with amusement, that when she asked him how he was getting on with the Indians, he replied: "All right. I know enough to talk to them. I know *halo* is yes, and *noitka*, no." Whereas the very reverse is the case!

These two years at Donald were broken by a short visit to his home in Ireland, owing to the need of rest and comfort after an attack of mountain fever; which is akin to ague. He landed in Ireland on January 13th, and sailed again for British Columbia on May 8th, 1889. We can see by the anecdotes related of his activities on behalf of his flock, that he had exerted his strength beyond the powers of the human body. Weak and overstrained, he returned to the dear home in Wicklow County, where his father and brothers welcomed and cared for him, till he recovered strength sufficient to enable his eager spirit to press on to the work once more.

CHAPTER VI
LETTERS

THE following letters from Mr Irwin relating to this period of his career, will illustrate what has been said, and give a clearer idea of the manner of his life and work:

"PRINCETOWN, SIMILKAMEEN,
"Saturday 19th, 1885.

"DEAR B. You will have been prepared no doubt for this heading by my last two letters. Here I am in the whirl of all kinds of excitement. First, as to the way I have got to this scene of action, f had a good ride on Friday week, from Kamloops, with Mr H., for about 38 miles, then we parted, he to Nicola, I to Douglas Lake. I put up with my friends the North of Ireland people, of whom I told you before. They were well and most kind; I baptized their child, and had some shooting, and started to the lake on Saturday afternoon; lost my way in the hills, and had quite a toss up as to where to go; however, as on Friday, I wandered about keeping a certain spot in view, and at last found myself at the right place. No notice had arrived about service; so I had to ride off round about and let them know I was there; darkish job, this, but I had a man with me who knew the way. Had service last Sunday there at n; good gathering. Afternoon rode 20 miles to Quilshana for evening service; good number. Englishman there, a wanderer; didn't see him afterwards. Slept with some friends at their nice house. Rode over to Nicola on Monday to find Mr H. very ill, dysentery; couldn't go on. Heavy rain prevented us camping out, so I had to make up my mind to ride through to Similkameen in the day, although it was a long ride. Started at 5 A.M. on Wednesday, having got up at 2.45, fed horse and got pack together, then off to awake an Indian who was to show me up the first 10 miles. He, poor chap, was asleep away down in his wigwam by a river, and it was a rum thing to find oneself out in the pitch dark morning searching for a tent across a horrid marsh, with a very spirited young mare four years old, then riding up to the tent and halloaing there till the sleep was broken and a voice from within crying out 'all right.' Then back I went and had a bite more breakfast, and was ready to be off in the biting cold breeze across the hills by an old trail. Indian showed me along till 6.30, then away I went, diving deep into unknown woods and the hills and streams ad lib., following an old trail of the Hudson Bay Co. that they had had in '46. I can't tell you all I should like to, as it would be endless. The autumn tints have begun. Cotton trees quite golden, and scarlet shrubs thrown out by the dark pines, and all reflected in the clearest of mountain lakes, will beat any pen. Then as we rode through the bush the birds added new glories to the scene. One thing you must hear of: after driving through the forest you come out on a whole chain of lakes, round which the trail winds until you get tired of their beauties; one of the lakes, called the Blue Lake, is the very loveliest thing I've ever seen. The water is just the colour of the blue or green round your old breakfast cups; some ore or mineral causes the whole thing simply to look like one big emerald crystal. I can't describe how heavenly it was; and then just in the right place was a great weed with bright scarlet leaves that showed off the wonderful colour to perfection. Though this was more lovely than the others, yet all had I heir own charms, and I can only-leave you to dream of endless lakes in a row, embedded in the finest fir-wood hills in the home of the deer and bear, and hardly broken by any but those feet who foot the trail not a house the whole way, and the whole day I didn't meet one single human soul, and I travelled some 50 odd miles along that trail. I think I accomplished the ride well, as it is a stiff one and seldom clone in less than two days. Camping out in the woods being the fashion here, little camp fires fringe the trail, and you can see how the big pines have their middles burnt out by the campers. Well! I had a near shave of being out myself all night, and I suppose I should have camped, if I had not a good deal of that Irish *Nil Desperandum* in my blood, as when I got down off the hills on to these flats near hero I could have given up myself for lost, as I knew Mr Allison's was on a river, and I was skirting a stream the whole time and yet never came to it; this was 6-30 to 7; it was pitch dark, but I chanced to meet a drunken Indian, who told me to keep the road, and so I did, but had to stick to it for 6 miles and then found myself on the brink of a steep bank ending in an Indian camp. The camp fire was blazing, and the Indians were all around their tents

eating and gambling; so I gave up all hope of more than an Indian
tent for the night. After halloaing and roaring at a fence round the
camp, a nice Indian came out and pointed out Allison's house some
few hundred yards away on the flat, so I was thankful, and had a
good supper and went to bed, rolled up in blankets in one corner of
a room. You would laugh to see me welcome the light of a house at
last; and I found the best of good friends here, and they have such a
comfortable place. On Wednesday I took it easy and went out with
the boys here to give my horse some bunch grass up the hills, such a
tear as we had. Now to get you into our shape here, I must let you
know how we are fixed. Nothing but mines and gold is heard of
here. The mines are just 12 miles away, but the men register here, so
we see hundreds. There are all sorts and conditions of men lawyers,
farmers, cowboys from the United States and Manitoba, a jolly lot of
rough cards, but rare good, fine-looking fellows and very hearty; and
then more than a thousand Chinamen. Such is the pack there on the
mines at Granite ('reek. It was Wednesday evening; just as we were
in the middle of supper I remember that an Indian, drunk and hurt,
came to get something from the store, but he was not given anything
at first, but like the widow he was stubborn and got a little
something to eat. He complained of a hurt. Well, we had just lighted
our pipes after supper and were sitting round the stove, when a
great knock came to the door and in came a queer crowd. Three
cowboys with clattering spurs, and armed to the teeth with revolvers
and rifles, came in with the terrible news of a man having been
murdered up at the mines. A rowdy lot were riding madly about the
camp and had been drinking, etc., when as one of the men was
swinging his revolver round his head and going about, he happened
to point it at the head of a friend of mine who was on a visit to the
mines; the ball struck him above the left eye, and it was the nearest
chance he wasn't killed on the spot. But this is going to the end
before you hear the exciting beginning of the story. Well! the three
boys who had come down from the mines reported the man "dead,
and they had started off amid a shower of bullets after the
murderers. They rode the 12 miles up and down hill in half an hour
they say. Then in our presence they were sworn in as constables, and
sent off to hunt down the shooter. All night they rode, but could not
get him, until late in the day they ran into him up at a farm in the

hills, and he made off on a good horse, but under threats of being shot he came back and gave himself up, and was run in here just before I left for the mines. He's a cowboy and a rough one. Joke is that the three constables are also cowboys, so you see how good they are on a case of this kind. He was committed, and is to go down to New Westminster to-morrow. They are going to take this letter down with them, so you see it will be quite romantic. You can guess how very sad I was to think that my friend had been shot, especially as he has a wife and family; and I should have gone up at once to see him if I had known the trail, but I had to put it off till next day. So on Thursday I started, and got upon a wretched beastly old screw of a horse that I was lent, and which I dragged up the hills and made him carry me down. Bah! I never was so sick in my life. However, we got into the camp at last, and there I was glad to see N. was all right and walking about. He had a terrible shave, and only escaped by a miracle; he was talking to some friends of mine as they were eating their supper, and had been laughing a minute before at the cook because he was afraid of the shooting, and next minute he was lying on his face on the ground. The cowboy at once made off whooping and yelling and was pursued by the others as you have heard. I had a nice time in the mining camp; lots of friends there, and had quite a number of visits to supper, etc. I shall have a service there to-morrow morning. The camp is in a big rough part of the country, and of course everything is terribly rough and ready; but it is not a bad place. A creek runs into the river and forms a peninsula, and on that tongue is the camp. The hills run up perpendicular on all sides and are well wooded. The tents are comfortable but a bit rough; no houses yet built, but some building; a whole forest was round about there, but now there are no trees hardly on the tongue, all having been felled to make mining implements, etc. The gold is plenty and I have seen lots of it; little wee pieces, as a rule, of all shapes, flat and bright; other big bits worth seventy-eight dollars or so, and others something less. Men get cracked on the subject, and no wonder; you could make your fortune in a morning if you had luck. It's a queer side of this rough life. I like the men, and they seem very nice as a rule. I wish though the whiskey was not in there; it is playing the fool with most of them. To-day we have had here another excitement; the Indians like the eagles are gathered together all round here from all parts. They got some whiskey here and were all drunk last night; so we ran some white men in and have been holding Court here. The Indian Chief being sorry for his poor people, came to give evidence, and he seems a fine sort of fellow; very unlike your picture chief, as he is dressed in ordinary Indian pants and shirt, and looks much like a back-woodsman with his long black hair and big moccassins. I was in fits of laughter as he was giving his evidence in Chinook, which is certainly an idiotic conglomeration. The real Indian is a mixture of clicks and chucks and gutterals, very like a bad sailor aboard ship, as he tries to repeat poetry to ease his soul and is sick at the same time.

"I must shut up now as I am hungry and it is lunch time, and this jobation is enough for at least four meals. Yours,

"HARRY."

"QUILSHANNA, NICOLA,
April, 1886.

"DEAREST M. I had some fairly rough days at the mines. The men have worked until the high water has driven them out, and have now to lie by for about six weeks till the ice and snow melt. It was by no means the best of roads or trails I had to travel over there. In fact, the very worst sort of walking for one whose feet are likely to be tender, as mine are still. Crawling along trails and sliding down ice slopes and scrambling up the steepest of precipices and all this in big top boots, you can fancy the state my feet were in. The skin was off most of them and the heels were all raw. On Sunday last I had morning service in camp, and then made a sharp walk to Otter Flat (six miles) and had afternoon service at three o'clock. Next morning I started on a bit longer tramp, as I could get no horse, shouldering my saddle bags, which were by no means light, I started about 8 A.M. for a big 30 mile tramp. People assured me at the start I could not possibly get over the creeks and rivers, which were swollen very high and even took the horses to swim them. However, my Irish nature won't give in, and I started. You can fancy me trudging along a good trail through the most lovely lake and forest scenery, up and down heavy hills, with saddle bags so arranged that one was on my chest and the other on my back, by slipping my head through the hole which fits on to the back of the saddle. I can tell you it was no easy pack I had. Well, I had a real good start and a most glorious walk on the finest of spring mornings. Ice on the lakes still and snow on the hills, but the warm sun makes those winter signs diminish quick. The birds are all hard at work, trying to make up for their tuneless nature by twittering in the maddest, merriest way. Blue jays little blue birds great white owls and hawks, with a lot of little brownies with black top knots, wild geese and ducks ad lib. on the lakes; a cayote here and there crawling about you can guess I enjoyed it well. Armed with a stout pilgrim's staff, I came to the first creek swollen high; this T crossed on a log, taking special pains to keep upright across the deepest part of the river, knowing that if I went in I should have fine times with the saddle bags round my neck! Well, then, I crossed a couple more creeks, successfully walking the logs, and that is no easy matter, as you have to balance yourself with your pole, which you can get to the upper side of the log, and the force of the current keeps it jammed to the log, and gives you a good support. But you would have seen, no doubt, a woeful expression on my face when I came to the next river, a perfect torrent boiling and fussing away in grand style, no log or tree to be seen anywhere. Well, off I went up stream to search for something, and at last came to a good stout tree; but it was three feet under water and a big rush going over it. This was my only chance; so I got on to it, and by dint of a little balancing, I astonished myself by getting safely across. You would have laughed to have seen me going inch by inch across the stream, taking just about five minutes to get across the thirty yards. I then walked on hard to the house of one of my friends, and there had lunch on beans and bacon, cooked out in a tent on a couple of logs, Indian fashion. It was a good scene for life in the Far West; a dirty, travelled-looking individual, a poor imitation of a parson, sitting at one side of the log fire; a tin plate with his bacon and beans on it, and his tinney of tea; bread just cooked on the fire in a dirty pan. The other leading figures being a dirty smutty looking coon, son of a

Canon, blackened with work and smoke: he was cook that clay. Dress, a pair of old gum boots, an old, very old shirt, and a beastly old pair of overalls as pants, completed his rig out. There were two Frenchmen besides him, who were even dirtier than he was. So you can form some idea of the Far West dirt. How grimy one gets to be sure! How you would have laughed to see me by the end of that 30 mile walk.

Excuse my plainness of speech, but we are and have to be very plain here. I got in to the half-way house all right in good time, best time on record for a pedestrian. A good night's sleep set me up, and yesterday morning I started with a German to walk right through here! That is, to finish up with 35 miles; we marched along from 7 to 6, with one and a half hour's rest in the middle of the day, and I got in here fairly beat last evening, but none the worse for the tramp, except that my feet are sadly in want of skin. I am taking it easy to-day, and hope to have a nice little ride this afternoon to the foot of the Nicola lake (about ten miles), which will set me up again. The mines and miners are the roughest part of this country just now. It is perfectly astonishing the numbers that have trooped in from all countries. It would do your heart good to hear some of the ghastly tales the old miners have of nearly every wild country of the globe; they are certainly the hardest, roughest, and yet best-hearted fellows alive. It has never been my lot to rub up against such an utterly fearless class of men. They go through the wildest countries in search of their darling gold, and no dangers daunt them. I could yarn for hours on their doings. Yours, H. I."

"BEAR CREEK, SELKIRKS, E.,
"March 8th, 1887.

"DEAREST B. I must write you a line to tell you of one of the most weird things you ever heard of and what I have just gone through to-day. A few days ago up here in the Selkirks an avalanche came thundering down Mount Carrol, and came right across the valley and struck the track, turned right up grade and smashed into two engines and the snow-plough, burying them completely, and sixteen men with them: nothing was to be seen of them but the end of the plough and the smoke stack of one engine and a spout of steam from the other engine, which was buried up altogether. Well, the slide came upon the men who were watching it come down the other side, before any of them could escape; of course when the few men who were around saw this, they set in digging and got out ten, but six of the poor fellows were killed; the men dared not go on digging for long, as avalanches were coming down all round them, and they were in peril of their lives. It was a strange scene and a heartrending one too; they no<y have got all the bodies out; one of them was the husband of a poor woman in Donald whom I know. I had to break the news to her, and as there was no one to hurry up things for her, I started for Donald yesterday, and after a ride of 12 miles on an engine, and then a run of 5 miles to catch another train up the hills, I got up to Bear Creek last evening late. This morning we had to start for the camp where the bodies were left, and I think of all queer frisks this day's was the greatest I ever had. We got about ten men to carry a coffin, and then away we went with avalanches coming down all round us; we had to run from one snowshed to another, keeping a good look out for the avalanches, the roars of which always told us when they came, and the flurry of snow ahead of them makes them exactly like artillery booming away, and the smoke curling from the guns; and, true to the simile, the great snow or ice balls come thundering down with all the frightful force of cannon balls. Well we had to climb over slides between the snowsheds, and that by a bad trail, over perhaps 30 feet of snow and trees, and you fancy that those 200 or 300 yards did not take us long to make. The scene of the accident was too awful and too weird to describe; all snow around piled up 100 feet, and there down in the hole the engines, and the graves of the poor six, one of whom we had to put in a coffin, and start back with along that fearful hillside, and run all the risks again. That was the strangest funeral procession that ever passed on earth; fancy avalanches rumbling and thundering around, and twelve men trailing across the hills with a coffin swinging on a pole; every man listening for the avalanche above him and going as fast as he could across the 200 yards between the sheds. I can tell you it made one

think of the six-hundred ride into the valley of death. However, thank God, we got through all safe, but we don't want to have to do it again. I am going in to Donald to-morrow with the coffin. Ever Yours,

"HARRY."

"DONALD,
"March 8th, 1887.

"DEAREST B. I had a fine time of it last Sunday getting that poor fellow's body down. I told you we had some horrid risks to run from the slides in carrying him across the hillside., and that was the weirdest funeral that the wildest imagination could paint; you can only think of great gigantic heights up to 4000 feet above you, and some 20 feet of snow on the hillsides; then you hear the rumbling like the rolls of thunder, you see the smoke (snow) rolling from guns and the slide rushes into the gulch below you at 100 miles a minute. No place can give you a better idea of the power of Nature and the powerlessness of man. There is no railroad to be seen; the only things to mark the line are the tops of telegraph poles, or the butt ends here and there where they have been turned endwise. Well, we felt most thankful to have escaped as we did, and when we returned you should have seen how pleased the boys were to see us back safe, as there were three great slides while we were away, and they came down just behind us; of course there is no chance of a man living if he is buried, as the slides will have to be blown out by powder; they are as solid as granite and just as heavy, in fact they are packed into ice. Well, Sunday morning I thought I could make down the hill to Donald, which was about 28 miles off. I had gangs of six men to help me to drag the coffin on a toboggan. I placed out three gangs and had to haul myself; and when not hauling I was breaking track through 3 feet of snow in the middle of the track. We toiled along at about 2 miles an hour, and about 4 P.M. met three engines ploughing their way through the snow up the hill. These picked us up on our way down, and helped us on about 8 miles. Then I wired for an engine from Donald, which came out and brought us in just by midnight; that was the hardest Sunday's work I've ever done, and hope it will be the last I'll have to do of that kind: of course I should not have done it unless the poor wife was here fretting her heart away that her husband's body was lying miles away in the snow. Hoping you will be out here some day to see the places that men can run such risks in. Love to all, your loving "HARRY."

CHAPTER VII
IN NEW WESTMINSTER, BRITISH COLUMBIA

IN the year 1890, the greatest happiness of Henry Irwin's life came to him, and also his greatest sorrow.

On January 8th, at the Church of S. Paul's, Esquimalt, Vancouver Island, his marriage was celebrated; the bride, as before said, was Miss Frances Stuart Innes, daughter of Mr J. H. Innes, Superintendent of H.M. Naval Establishment at Esquimalt. Her sister, Mrs Shildrick says: "Mr Irwin was then domestic chaplain to the late Bishop Sillitoe, and assistant priest at Holy Trinity Cathedral. The husband and wife were devoted to each other." The young couple settled in the city of New Westminster, in a pretty little house on the main street which runs parallel with the Eraser River, and on its bank.

New Westminster, known in the Far West as "The Royal City," because the name was given to it by the good Queen Victoria, is a very beautiful town, where one feels it is good to dwell. Carved out from the primeval forest, which still remains to some extent us an adornment to the higher levels of the town, it. forms as it were a series of terraces parallel with the Eraser River, intersected by extremely steep streets leading upwards from the main street and the railway track.

Hitherto, the Bishop had lived in Sapperton, a suburb of New Westminster, and ministered in the church there, Archdeacon Woods being Rector of Holy Trinity, New Westminster. But now the Bishop assumed the charge of Holy Trinity, which thus became a Cathedral Church. It was, however, in addition to the episcopal visitations throughout the diocese, too great a burden for the Bishop's strength, already undermined by ten years of arduous work as a colonial Bishop, with constant harassing anxiety concerning ways and means; for in spite of the noble generosity of the S.P.G., and the loyal efforts of his committee at home, funds came in far too slowly and in too meagre a supply for the needs of the clergy in the diocese, for whom the heart of their Father in God often bled.

The Bishop entered on his new duties on July 19th, 1889, and the Rev. H. Irwin became assistant curate a week later. The old rectory was demolished to make way for the present commodious See House, Bishop and Mrs Sillitoe still living at Sapperton, a mile and a half away, in a pretty wooden dwelling somewhat like a chalet, and in a large garden, bright with shrubs and flowers. This is the old Archdeaconry House, and is close to the little church at Sapperton thus described by the Bishop:

"S. Mary's Church stands in the grounds of the Archdeaconry House, and is a model of what all wooden churches might be and ought to be. It was designed and built by the sappers who came out on the original expedition under Colonel Moody. It was the 'fashionable church' of those days. Government House stood near; officials and their staff had their residences round about; an English tone pervaded the little society, and they took pride in the church they had built for themselves and in its services."

The Bishop's first impressions of New Westminster, are interesting and still very exact:

"This is really a very lovely place, though of course we have the advantage of the first fresh brilliancy of summer to heighten its natural beauty; but the whole situation is well chosen and picturesque. The ground rises suddenly from the river on both banks, so that in the town the houses stand one above another; every one has a view, and indeed a view more or less panoramic, since abundance of space has given nearly every house a garden. The opposite bank of the river is covered with pine forest, rising suddenly to about a hundred feet above the stream; and over this ridge, from the higher parts of the town, is seen the snowy summit of Mount Baker, nearly 70 miles away to the south-east. Down the river, to our right, about a mile distant, two fir-clad islands divide the stream into three great arms and form a basin just above them fully two miles wide, across which we look over to the mountains of

Vancouver Island; while up stream to our left, the view is bounded by the mountains of the Cascade range, thirty miles off, and still, at mid-summer, largely covered with snow." ["Church Work in British Columbia," by the Rev. H. Gowen (Longmans).]

There is but little that we can say of the home life of Mr and Mrs Irwin. For the young wife there would be much to do to make and keep the home bright and cosy. Servants are rare in the Far West, and gentlewomen are not afraid to do the necessary work of their own houses. And then there came brighter hopes still to occupy her. A few words from Mrs Greswolde Williams, formerly a resident in British Columbia, speaks of this time:

"Mr Irwin was essentially an Irishman. His impulsive disposition and love of adventure were genuinely Irish, and that is the key to his character.

"I have heard him say he came to Canada fully resolved to remain a celibate and devote himself entirely to missionary work. But he met Miss Inacs, and the ideals of his life somewhat changed, though a missionary he remained to the end.

"All who knew him in New Westminster knew also his intense devotion to his wife, a devotion that remained unchanged till his death."

Shall we not say that the very transience of this precious time added to the permanence of its impression? Happy, indeed, and few are those who in their lives can find the memory of a period which perfect love and perfect sympathy have enriched. With the Irwins it was so; the wife's tender grace still remains a pathetic memory, the husband's chivalrous devotion a treasured one, among their friends in the Far West.

And then, sadly, quickly, came the end. A little one who never drew breath in this world; the young mother taken three days after, and the husband and father left alone in the house which had seen so much happiness.

The following letter from Mrs Sillitoe who was ever so true a friend to Mr Irwin, will best tell the sad and simple story:?

"You ask me to tell you what I can about Mr Irwin's short married life, and the time afterwards that he spent at the See House as the Bishop's Secretary and Chaplain.

"Being away from all my papers it is impossible for me to remember exact dates, but I think it was about the New Year 1890 that Mr Irwin brought his bride to New Westminster, to a little house not far from the Church, and which years before had been used for Columbia College, the girls' school, which was opened soon after the Bishop reached the Diocese.

"Father Pat and his wife were like two children in the delight they took in everything, in the pride they took in each other and their cosy little home; and although it was given them to spend so short a time together here below, that time was one of unclouded happiness. This I say from observation and from what Mr Irwin has since told me, for he loved to talk to me of his wife and of their happiness, telling me all sorts of little anecdotes of their life.

"The All Saints' Day services, the anniversary Festivals of the Diocese of New Westminster, were always much observed, the Choral Evensong the day before being attended by many from Vancouver and other parishes; and at the Choral Celebration on the Festival itself there was always an unusually large congregation.

"At the Choral Evensong of All Saints' Eve 1890, the hymn, 'For all the Saints who from their labours rest,' was sung for the first time. Mrs Irwin was not feeling well enough to attend the service, but walked over to the Cathedral to listen from outside. She. thought she had never heard anything more beautiful than this hymn, the beauty of which lifts us for a while above the small worries and harassments of earth, the last triumphant verses carrying us almost into the Divine Presence. 'And to think,' as Mr Irwin said to me so soon afterwards, 'that it should have been sung for her.'

"The little baby whose advent was to fill up the cup of happiness already so full, was not permitted to see the light of this world; and on the evening of a Sunday in November, on which so many prayers had been offered for the safety of mother and child, the little body was laid at rest in a corner of the beautiful cemetery overlooking the Fraser River and snowclad mountains beyond. The grave is now marked by a tiny stone on which is a touching inscription.

"Three days later Mrs Irwin died, the shock being all the more crushing as she was supposed to be recovering. On the evening of the funeral, Mr Irwin took up his residence at the See House, and here he stayed until early in 1894, when he was called to Ireland, a few months before the Bishop's death, on account of his father's severe illness.

"Of his work during these years there is not much to be recorded. It consisted of the humdrum everyday drudgery, the writing and copying of letters, interviews, parochial work (for he was curate of the Cathedral), and numberless other things too insignificant to mention.

"The office, a large room in the See House used for meetings and the transactions of business, was where he was usually to be found, although he had a private sitting room. In the evenings he was surrounded by a number of young fellows, for the most part either strangers or down on their luck.

"Our Sunday evening suppers at the See House were always motley gatherings of all sorts and conditions of men; frugal meals they were, as indeed was all our fare; but happy and restful after the day's work was over. It was a great amusement to Father Pat to tell us afterwards of the remarks that were made, the great simplicity being so different from what was supposed to be *en règle* in an episcopal household.

"Mr Irwin's sunny disposition made him a charming member of the family, and the love between him and the Bishop was more that of a father and son, and in all these years I never remember any friction dimming its brightness.

"Mr Irwin always believed the best of everyone, and his character was to strangers a misleading one: he was so sweet tempered, so anxious to think others right and to yield his own way, that people were inclined to think that he could be easily led and influenced; and it was only when they were brought up against his principles that they found themselves face to face before a solid wall round which there was no way of getting. When he felt a thing to be right, there was no shadow of yielding. He was from the first one of my truest and dearest friends; but although I knew he was out of health, I had no idea that the end, for which he so much longed, was so near. The sorrow for my personal loss could not but be very great, and yet there was happiness in knowing that his many and arduous labours were over, and that in the Rest of Paradise he was re-united to those loved ones gone before. Believe me, sincerely yours,

"VIOLET G. SILLITOE."

In a corner of the beautiful little cemetery at Sapperton is a semi-circular headstone, very low and small. In its centre is a sacred symbol, the Cross enclosed in a circle. It is the grave of the nameless little one who never saw the light; and beneath the symbol are these touching lines:

> "No name had I, O Christ, to offer Thou.
> Nor from Thy font received the sacred sign;
> Yet in Thy Book of Life remember me.
> I plead my Saviour's Name instead of mine."

"CHILD OF H. AND J. S. IRWIN."

Not far off lie the parents in one grave, with two white marble crosses at head and foot.

CHAPTER VIII
A QUIET TIME

A LINE of black was, as it were, drawn across Henry Irwin's life at this time; and though his friends tell us that the zest of life was still abundant in him, and that in his work he was ever more and more brave and bright, yet we can note an underlying secret sorrow gnawing at his heart. It showed itself in a restless desire of motion, of hard work; a longing to throw himself heart and soul, and body too, into the roughest, meanest toil for his brethren. He covered his grief from strangers with utter shrinking from observation, even with simulated indifference. When one who had not yet heard of his loss asked him: "How is Mrs Irwin" he replied with a sort of laugh, "Oh! did you not know, she died last week?" and turned away. Can we not catch an echo of that laugh, sadder than any tears?

The kindness of the Bishop and Mrs Sillitoe was beyond words. Mr Arthur Irwin says:?

"During the sad time after his wife's death, the kindness of the Bishop and Mrs Sillitoe was past comprehension, and from that time forward the Bishop treated him as a son and gave him rooms in the See House."

In 1891, he paid a second visit to his home in Ireland, landing on January 30th and sailing again on May 1st. This visit was a sorrowful one, being so soon after his wife's death. Bishop Sillitoe persuaded him to take this change in order to recover his mental tone. It seems to have helped him to do so to some extent, yet his wife was never absent from his thoughts. He would speak of her as "Fanny," exactly as if he expected her to come into the room at any moment.

No one, hearing him speak of her and ignorant of the facts, would imagine that she was dead. Her friends were specially dear to him.

Henry Irwin returned from his short visit home, refreshed and ready for his work as secretary to Bishop Sillitoe.

The life in the new See House, of which Mr Irwin was now an inmate, was happy, simple, and, though homely, much more comfortable in the spacious airy rooms of the handsome wooden building than had been the case in the pretty but small house at Sapperton. In this latter residence, the Bishop and Mrs Sillitoe had been honoured by a visit from the Princess Louise, and her husband the Marquis of Lorne, when on a tour as Governor-General of Canada. They joined in the home life with kindly simplicity.

In the company of his kind and fatherly friend the Bishop, Mr Irwin remained till January 1894, during which time church work in the diocese continued to make steady progress. At the end of 1890 three experienced priests, Mr Croucher, Mr Edwardes and Mr (now Archdeacon) Small, had left the diocese with a view to other work. Their places were hard to fill, especially that of Mr Small, among the Indians at Lytton, British Columbia. In vain the Bishop sent home earnest appeals for a man to come and work among this interesting people; but a school for Indian girls at Yale, British Columbia, under Sisters from Ditchingham in Norfolk, was making progress, and proving what invaluable work it was possible for Christian women to do among their Indian sisters. With this school Father Pat had to do; it was the chief item of his work for the Indians. A new wing had been built to this school at a cost of about £700, of which the Dominion Government gave £300. On December 29, 1890, the Bishop and Mrs Sillitoe went to Yale, and the new-wing of the school was dedicated by a procession; the Bishop in cope and mitre was preceded by Aimie, a little half-breed girl of twelve, as cross-bearer, dressed like all her confirmed companions, in white veil and red pinafore. Another child came after the Bishop carrying the school banner; then four choir children, then the remainder of the school, the Sisters, and finally a troop of Indians. These last, nearly seventy in number, walked in couples and in reverent order and silence. Upstairs wound the long procession, numbering just 100 in all, singing the 67th Psalm ("God be merciful unto us and bless us"), then downstairs again to the refectory and schoolroom, suitable prayers and responses being said in each, ending with a short service in the little chapel where there was hardly standing room. A Christmas Tree followed, and then a magic lantern show of scenes embracing the chief English cathedrals: a red-letter day indeed for the Indians of Vale.

In July 1905 the writer visited the spot. After a hot night in the train, the early morning freshness at Yale was very acceptable, and also the kind welcoming faces of the Vicar and of a lady from the school. Little dark-skinned Indian girls from the village, clad in red cotton and holding Indian baskets with cherries, offered the fruit for sale to the passengers; and very refreshing were the cherries to our parched lips.

A short walk by the Eraser brought us to the school., where a charming welcome from the Sister in charge awaited us. After a rest, we took a walk with some of the Indian girls by the river, which here is deep and rapid and swirls along between romantic mountains clothed with verdure almost to the top. We sat by a brooklet the girls' favourite spot which rippled on under fern and moss on its way to the river, and we chatted and told stories and had a happy time. We received an Indian basket from them as a parting gift, and we highly value it as a memento of a happy visit.

There is no doubt that the work done in this school, and in that for Indian boys at Lytton, British Columbia, lately built and endowed by the New England Society and under the care of the Rev. G. Ditcham, is the best foundation for the evangelization of this interesting people in the diocese, by training them to form Christian homes and found Christian families, with habits of decency and order. We owe a debt to the Indian race, and in no way can we pay it better than by aiding such efforts at civilization on the only true basis, namely, the Christian religion.

In all such work Mr Irwin of course took part, though as we have, seen the Indian language was not his forte. He had yet to find out the direction in which his work was to prove so striking and unique.

In 1892, Bishop Sillitoe was attacked by influenza a serious attack, from the effects of which he never fully recovered. It began in February; and though he was able to be out of doors early in March, a relapse followed, and he was obliged to rest from time to time. Still, he went over the greater portion of his diocese in that year, including three visits to Nelson, now the chief town and headquarters of the Church in Kootenay. It is the important centre of a large and growing mining district, beautifully situated at the head of the Kootenay Lake. The work in the diocese went on steadily, and a beginning was made in the mission to the Chinese in Vancouver and New Westminster a most important work. Thousands of Chinese flock to British Columbia for labour of various kinds; in laundry, gardening, and cooking they excel; and as there are few female servants, the Chinese are invaluable in a domestic capacity. Bishop Sillitoe and Bishop Dart have expressed their deep sense of the obligation laid on Christians in British Columbia to work for the conversion of the Chinese in their midst while absent from their own land, with its temptations and hindrances to Christianity.

A Chinese catechist from Honolulu, S. Ten Yong, began a class in Vancouver; and many friends, first among whom we must name Mrs Greswolde Williams, assisted in furthering the work there and in New Westminster. Bishop Sillitoe had two Chinese servants in his own household.

So quietly and busily passed the time throughout 1892 and 1893. Father Pat was with those who loved and cared for him; he enjoyed his rooms in the See House, and had the privilege of bringing a friend to dinner; and many were the jokes at his expense concerning his use of this privilege; for he was always on the "losing side," and not seldom introduced to the Bishop's table some poor fellow "down on his luck," whom such a reminder of better days might console and encourage. But he was careful before doing so, to hire a suit of fitting clothes for his protege, and not to encroach too far on the hospitality of Mrs Sillitoe.

Meanwhile, a change was impending in the happy Irish home. In July, 1892, Mr Irwin's father had a serious apoplectic attack, and the medical attendant had such grave fears of another equally sudden seizure, that Mr Arthur Irwin invented a code of telegraphic communication with his brother Henry. In December 1893 the dreaded attack came, and the word "Hyac" (Chinook for Hurry) was cabled to Father Pat. The Bishop kindly allowed him to start at once, and he arrived at home on January 8th, 1894, little thinking that he would never again see the Father in God who had been so true a comforter in his sorrow.

Mr Irwin's father recovered slowly, and up to June 1894, Father Pat assisted in the parish and church, relieving his father of work and anxiety.

On July ii he received tidings of Bishop Sillitoe's death, which came to him as a great shock, and he mourned for him as a son.

The Bishop, as before stated, had never thoroughly recovered from the effects of influenza; and though at the beginning of 1894 he felt stronger and better, his friends were still anxious, and the English committee offered to pay all expenses if he would take the needed rest. The secretary, Mr Mogg, writes: "His answer overflowed with gratitude, but he pointed out the "difficulties of leaving, and continued: 'I cannot go away until I have given the parishes the opportunity of confirmations. . . . We must try and make up for the falling-off last year. Again, I do not think I need go away for six months. I am now very well; my only trouble some symptoms in my heart; but quiet and, above all, peace of mind, are the best relief for this.' "

He went on bravely with his episcopal duties, but gave up the incumbency of the Cathedral Church, Holy Trinity, New Westminster, to which the Rev. A. Shildrick was appointed Rector, while the West End of the city had now become a district that of S. Barnabas under Mr Gowen, with a neat church of its own. Mr Croucher had succeeded Father Pat as domestic chaplain.

While at Lytton, the headquarters of the Indian work, on Whit-Sunday, 1894, though feeling ill and worn out, Bishop Sillitoe braced himself to give to his Indian converts the precious boon of Confirmation. He came to the Indian church at 8.50 A.M., supported by Mrs Sillitoe, went through the service, and spoke briefly but to the point to the newly confirmed. This was his last episcopal act. On Whit-Monday he left for Yale, and the end came rapidly. He endured terrible suffering at Yale, whispering prayers between the awful struggles for breath. On Sunday, May 27, as he sat in his bedroom in the parsonage at Yale, adjoining the little wooden church, he could follow the service heard through the open window. Mrs Sillitoe, of course, was with him.

A flood, owing to the rapid rise of the Eraser from melting snow in the mountains, was causing grave anxiety at this time; the lower part of Yale was under water, and wooden houses went sailing swiftly down the river. The knowledge of his people's sufferings added to the Bishop's trouble, but when on June 1 he started for home on a river steamer, he seemed to bear the journey well. Soon after his arrival at home he received the Holy Communion at the hands of Mr Croucher, and then lapsed into unconsciousness. Incessant prayers were offered to God on his behalf, and on the Saturday night he calmly breathed his last. The telegraphic message sent home was: "Bishop asleep," and thus a holy and good spirit passed to a better world, and one phase of Church work in British Columbia was ended.

CHAPTER IX
A NEW BEGINNING

IN less than four months after the death of Bishop Sillitoe, Henry Irwin was to bear the loss of his beloved father, the Reverend Henry Irwin, for thirty-one years incumbent of the chapel-of-ease at Newtown, Mount Kennedy, in Ireland. The loss of a dear and honoured parent creates a chasm in a man's life. On that side are all the dear memories of childhood and of the dear and cherished companionship; on this side, cold and silence.

Struck down by pneumonia on September the fifteenth, Mr Irwin lingered till S. Matthew's Day (September 21, 1894), and then slept away into rest. The funeral was impressive, and a memorial sermon was preached by the Reverend Canon Robinson on the text: "Blessed are they that dwell in Thy House." In God's House indeed this venerable man had ever dwelt; his own home had been a house of God, and the church was his dearest home of all: there he taught his flock, old and young, the simple gospel truths, and there he gathered his people to receive the Bread of Life.

Father Pat had been away from his home for a time before his father's death, obeying an urgent summons to help his former Rector, Mr Murray, who was in failing health. Those who saw him at Rugby, and had known him there as a curate, a bright, young fellow, fresh from Oxford, somewhat fastidious in dress and habits, felt that they were in the presence of another being. Even on his first visit in 1888 a change was noticed. His brother says: "He left home in 1885, a smooth-faced, youthful-looking priest of the true Anglican type: he arrived home, two years and eight months later, looking twenty years older, with whiskers and moustache, and sallow hardened skin, speaking with a somewhat nasal twang," and with a pointed beard which he used laughingly to allude to as his Saving Point.

Now, in addition, there were the results of the blow that had fallen upon him in his wife's death. Although that loss was always present to him, and he carried always with him a copy of In Memoriam, from its exquisite pages gathering consolatory thoughts, yet he did his best to set his grief aside, and to see God's providence even in the blow. But it had hewn a fresh model from the marble of his nature, and the Father Pat known to the miners would never have been but for that loss.

After his father's death (having been summoned from Rugby on the approach of that calamity) Henry Irwin stayed at Newtown and carried through another work, that of converting the small chapel-of-ease into a church with a parish. Up to the end of 1895, Father Pat's work was to see to the conversion of this church, with its trust funds, into the constitution of a parish, and the dedication and consecration of it as S. Matthias' Church, Newtown, Mount Kennedy. "Having completed these matters to the satisfaction of all concerned, he saw the appointment of a revered clergyman to the vacant cure before his departure again for British Columbia on January 8th, 1896, exactly two years from the date of his landing in 1894." [From a letter by A. W. Irwin, Esq.]

Meanwhile a new Bishop had been appointed to the vacant see of New Westminster. After certain difficulties in the Colonial Synod, which delayed the selection, the choice was relegated to the Archbishop of Canterbury and his assessors, and fell on the Rev. John Dart, who had earned a valuable experience in Ceylon under Bishop Chapman, and as head of the Theological College in Nova Scotia, where he had married a Nova Scotian lady of great personal charm; and at the time of his appointment to the see, he was acting as S.P.G. deputation in the Diocese of Manchester. At the close of 1895, he went out to his new diocese, where great trials, financial and personal, awaited him, to be met with a firmness and judicious patience that are the strong characteristic of this prelate.

Soon after Bishop Dart reached his new diocese, Mr Irwin wrote to him to propose returning thither. The Bishop from the first fully appreciated the noble and self-denying enthusiasm of the man; and their intercourse from first to last was marked by an affectionate regard on the part of the superior and elder, by a beautiful respect and confidence on the part of the younger, as testified in each of the letters from Mr Irwin, carefully preserved by Bishop Dart, several of which with his permission are reproduced here.

It was Mr Irwin's wish to devote himself from the date of his return to British Columbia, to good hard work of the pioneer sort; and accordingly the Bishop appointed him as Mission Priest to Rossland, then a rapidly growing mining district in the lonely mountainous country in the south of the diocese, in that half of it nearer the Rocky Mountains and known as Kootenay.

In 1896 Mr Carlyle, Minister for Mines, in his annual report says: "Early in the sixties, the placer mines on Wild Horse, Findlay, and other creeks in East Kootenay, having been discovered, resulted in the rush there of miners, and the constant demand for supplies,, as there was no means of communication between the coast and this district, except through the United States, with vexatious delays at the Customs."

Mr E. Dewdney, afterwards the Lieutenant-Governor of British Columbia, was instructed to survey and construct a trail entirely within British territory, through the southern part of the province, as a passage to the north had proved to be not feasible. In 1865 this trail, since known as the Dewdney Trail, was finished, and in its course it passed about one mile south of the present town of Rossland on its way down Trail Creek to the Columbia River.

The town is now approached by a branch railway, which zigzags most picturesquely up the mountain pass. It joins at Robson the main C.P.R. line over the Crow's Nest Pass.

The mines were found to be rich in ores yielding iron, copper, silver and gold. The chief mines are the Le Roi, the War Eagle, the Centre Star, the Virginia, and the Idaho; all gracious names, but alas! the things they represent are unlovely enough. As Mrs Browning says of other scenes:

"The palpitating engines snort and steam across the acres, And mark upon the blasted heaven the ruin of the land."

When ever did a mine not blight the natural beauty of a landscape Here in the purest of air, on a high tableland overlooking a luxuriant landscape, the rough shacks of the miners, the gaunt engines and black waste of the mines, are as blots before the eye.

Father Pat did not ask for beauty; he only asked for work, and he got it. He settled down among his people only bent on their good, absolutely forgeful and negligent of his own welfare. His flock was of most varied character. An eye-witness says: "Rossland is eminently cosmopolitan. There were men of all European nationalities, as well as Americans and Chinese. The mining fever had seized them all; but how differently it affected them! There may be seen the pig-tailed Chinaman, fanning himself as he saunters in his soft white shoes along the pavement, his objects and occupations a deep mystery, but certain to be involved in money-getting, his poorer brother bending under a load of the barbarian's dirty linen, with his pigtail twisted for convenience round his greasy brow. There are 'the boys' back from the mines, with 'a good rough on them,' determined to enjoy the town. There is the German, the plump Jew, the Yankee. Men everywhere in abundance standing in knots at street corners, sitting outside the hotels or bars, or perched in armchairs, having their boots cleaned in the thoroughfare; and all this crowd, no matter what other ostensible object they might have, had but one craze the mines. [Frances Macnab, in "British Columbia for Settlers" (Chapman & Hall).]

"Yet there was want and suffering here sometimes. The prospectors, who love the hills with an instinct that is more sporting than mercenary, are, for the most part, an improvident race; and if they come back, as many of them do, having found nothing, they return to suffer want. [A Prospector is a man who goes about among the mountains to discover ore. He keeps his discoveries secret till he can find a capitalist to buy his information.] They will help each other to a dinner, but if times are bad with many at once, even this resource may become exhausted. They are distinctly not the men to whom charity could be offered; and if assistance, is given by anyone outside the charmed circle of their own set, it must be done most delicately. I was delighted to find in 'Father Pat' (the English clergyman at

Rossland) one who thoroughly appreciated and liked the miners and prospectors; a feeling which, I believe, was warmly reciprocated by them. As I walked with him in Rossland, I occasionally overheard scraps of conversation which, perhaps, were not intended for me.

"'Why, Dick! did I see you in church this evening? '

"'Yes, yer reverence, I was there. The first time for thirty years. I couldn't stand too much of it at a time, though. So just when it was getting a bit long I went outside and had a smoke. I say, yer reverence, it was good! I went in again after I'd had a bit of a smoke, and it all came back to me as I was used to it when I was a boy, and I tell ye I did come down on them ah-mens! '

"When I was in Rossland, Father Pat was busy establishing a free library and sitting-room, which he had artfully contrived under the floor of the church. Many a time had we to perambulate down the hillside to admire this library.

"'A person don't have to belong to my church or Sunday-school,' said Father Pat, delivering his invitations as he went along, 'or any Sunday-school, to be welcome. Doors are always open books, magazines, are there. All that anyone has to do is to help himself. There are comfortable chairs. I want those young men and others who have no places and no homes to go to.'

"It was instructive to hear Father Pat discourse upon human nature. He was best at this when he sat in the open doorway of the shack in which he chose to reside. The shack, like the library, was always open. 'My experience in this Western country,' he would say, 'is that the more you trust human nature, and treat people like fellow beings, and not with suspicion, the better you will like them. If I knew a man was a born thief, I would throw the doors open to him and trust him just the same, relying on his better nature not to betray me. Take my advice, young man,' he cried, as a smartly dressed youth in Sunday best was passing, 'and don't be too suspicious of your fellow mortals, especially if they be dressed in overalls and boots. Rather beware of kid gloves and perfumed clothes.'

"The young man thus addressed started and turned his head. On seeing Father Pat, he raised his hat and beamed a silent benediction, and went on his way.

"Possibly Father Pat carries his ideas farther than need be. I was obliged sometimes to remonstrate, but the men understood him. 'He's a good man,' said one. 'We know that. There's nothing we can give him. His reward is ready for him, for all the poor fellows he's nursed and cared for that nobody else would bother about. No one can take it from him. He's recorded his claim right enough.'"

Though time works rapid changes in that quickly-shifting country, and men are soon forgotten, yet to this day stories are rife about the beloved Father Pat of the miners, and long may his name be green there as "a spray of Western pine." When Bishop Dart made his first visitation it was a rough road he travelled on to get there: he described it as "a journey in the air with an occasional rest on the seat," such were the bumps of his springless conveyance over the roads often formed of logs laid side by side. He found Father Pat cosy enough in those rooms under the church which were intended for his use, and which, as we see above, he turned eventually into a reading-room. On the Bishop's second visit a poor homeless prospector was ensconced there, and Father Pat had betaken himself to the wretched shack which he henceforth called his home. Could my readers see that shack they would realize what such self-denial meant to a cultured gentleman. A small hut of boards, with rough, uneven wooden steps climbing up a mud bank to the door; the whole in a side alley near the church turned away from all the fine prospect of hill and valley. And yet this seemed to him too great a luxury to enjoy alone; for he constantly had some sick or needy man to share it with him. As to clothes, he adopted the blue Derry of the miners as his working costume. There is a story of a young fellow fresh from England, who brought an introduction to the Rev. H. Irwin, and who on finding the shack, and its occupant clad in the rough dress of a miner, went away, certain that he had mistaken the place and the man.

The more civilized part of his wardrobe was constantly being diminished by the inroads of his reckless charity. He simply could not keep a good hat or coat or pair of boots for himself, when another needed them. It is told that when his congregation became scandalized by the green and threadbare overcoat he wore, they summoned up courage to remonstrate, and begged him to accept a new and warm one which they would provide, better suited to the severe weather. He thanked them heartily and accepted the gift with affectionate gratitude. For a few days he appeared in the grand new coat and expressed his appreciation of its warmth and comfort. But alas! it was not long before the new coat disappeared, and the old green and threadbare one took its place again. "Where is your new coat, Father Pat" they asked. "What have you done with it?" A look of contrition came over his face, as he answered:

"Well, what could I do? I met a poor fellow who had no overcoat at all. I couldn't let him go without one in this bitter weather, and I couldn't give him my old one, could I?" A similar tale is recorded of a new hat; and I was told that once, gazing on a scarecrow in a field, he said jokingly, but with absolute justice, that he might change hats with it with advantage to himself.

His days and nights were given to others. His door was ever open to the men. They might smoke with him, chat with him; and then, in the confidence of such talk, he would lead many a poor fellow to confess his faults, to ask advice, to remember the better life past, the prayers and counsels learned at a mother's knee. Who can tell what such quiet talks among the tobacco-smoke in the rough shack may have done for many a soul?

The wooden church of Rosslanol is a barnlike erection standing on a small piece of level land on the slope on which Rossland lies. It is below the roadway, below the shops and houses. One goes down a ricketty wooden stairway to it. As is the custom in the Far West, rooms are beneath it, intended (as beforesaid) for the clergyman's use, but given up by him for the parish. The church is perfectly plain in form, a simple rectangle, but a chancel is contrived by a wooden screen, and everything in this extemporized sanctuary is "decent and in order." The evening services are especially good and earnest, and the voluntary choir do their work well.

Such was the church where Father Pat ministered, and such it still is; but a new one will, it is hoped, be shortly erected under the auspices of the present Vicar, the Rev. H. W. Simpson.

A few extracts from the Rossland Parish Magazine of this date, with a diary written by Father Pat himself, may fitly close this chapter:?

"H. Irwin arrived in Rossland from England on January 27, 1896, and having secured the Opera House for service, held mission services on February 2nd, and also went to Trail in the afternoon, but was late, owing to the breakdown of an ore team which blocked the road for the ore wagon on which he was travelling. [Trail is a small town at the foot of the track which descends the hill from Rossland.]

"The absence of books made it necessary to print both hymns and canticles; and this expense, with the rent of the Opera House, made it necessary for him to turn out of the hotel into a shack with four other men for two months, by which time, with the ready help of a Ladies' Guild, the work of building a church for Rossland took shape.

"On May 1st, the first visit to the Kettle River District was paid, and services were held on May 3rd at Grand Forks, where lots were secured for the church.

"On returning to Rossland, two lots were offered for church building purposes, and a subscription list opened with fifty subscribers, a legacy from Bishop Sillitoe, and contributions from S.P.C.K. and Mr Lloyd Graeme, in memory of his son who died in Rossland, completing the amount required to build.

"On May 29th, church lots were secured at Trail, and a foundation was shovelled out on June 2 and 3.

"Bishop Dart paid his first visit to Rossland on August 16. A building committee was then appointed, and the work of building and furnishing proceeded with; and the first services were held in our own building at Christmastide with great joy."

The church at Rossland is connected in my mind with an amusing incident. One Sunday evening in August 1905, I attended the service, which was warm and hearty, the building being full to suffocation. It so happened that a Friendly Society named The Brethren of Pythias was that evening attending in state. The Archdeacon of Kootenay, who was officiating, had by some accident not been informed of this fact till he issued from the vestry at the head of the choir. When he began his sermon he expressed a warm welcome to the Brethren, regretting that, not having known of their intention to be present in a body, he was unable to give them an address specially prepared, but he hoped that the one he was about to give would prove suitable and acceptable. He then gave out his text: "Lo! these that have turned the world upside down, are come hither also."

CHAPTER X
SNAP-SHOTS

WHEN we were in Kootenay, indeed, I may say, in any part of British Columbia, the name of Father Pat was one to conjure with. The face of our interlocutor would light up as we spoke, and a flood of anecdote would pour forth. He was a hero in the land.

An interesting account of him is given by the Reverend Charles Ault Procunier, an ex-Methodist minister, now Rector of the important town of Revelstoke, British Columbia.

"When I first met 'Father Pat' (he says), I was an ex-minister of 'The Methodist Church of Canada,' having resigned from the membership and ministry of that religious society for the express purpose of becoming a candidate for Holy Orders in the Church of England. His Lordship, the Bishop of New Westminster, who had made all arrangements for my ordination to the Diaconate in Victoria, British Columbia, by the Bishop of Columbia, on June the 5th, 1898, was in England. At this important time appeared the inevitable flaw in mundane affairs. The ordination was postponed. However, after voluminous telegrams and letters the ordination was again arranged, the time June the 22, 1898, the place S. George's, Rosslands, and the Bishop was The Rt. Rev. Lemuel Henry Wells, Bishop of Spokane.

"On June the 21st I arrived, with my young son, who was five years old his mother was in the hospital in Kaslo, British Columbia on the train at 11.30 P.M., and as I stepped out of the train crowded with a Western populace miners, speculators, gamblers, etc. the circle of my life, for the first time, touched the invisible circle of the deep life of 'Father Pat.'

"'Hello, Procunier, old boy,' were his unconventional so words. There was no red-tape of social forms, no conventional snobbishness, but a man with a human heart. As his guest at the Lancaster Club I was lodged; and while we had a quiet glass of Scotch whisky and a soothing pipe, late though it was, there was a steady flow of wit and wisdom, humour and advice, which I shall never forget. But, however, the conclusion was practical details and arrangements for the future.

"On the following day, in his church, the Confirmation and Ordination took place. Then came his practical insight for specific details. Having a innate inclination for missionary work, he had long desired a favourable opportunity to visit the various mining camps and towns, which were springing into existence like blades of grass in the spring, and, behold! here was the chance. I was left in charge of S. George's Parish, Rossland. The difficult task of his Church work was, with fear and trembling, undertaken. In my quiet moments of higher insight, I have sometimes questioned his objective interest in the wild ways of mining camps at that particular time. Was it not rather pure self-sacrifice and self-denial, in order that he might provide an open door to organized work, and an infallible income for a raw 'tenderfoot' as they say in the West in the Church?

"However, he was a true missioner, and a tried exemplar of the profound principle of practical Christianity. If God speaks to us in nature, in history, in conscience, and in Revelation, most assuredly, in his saintly life, there was heard the 'small still voice' of God. It was his feasible advice, open church and free hand, that made the rugged path of my life smooth and plain.

"Thus with his hand to my hand, and heart to my heart, we laboured until the missionary district of Fort Steele, British Columbia, was opened, and all arrangements had been completed for my incumbency there. Again, into conspicuous prominence came his noble traits. He must needs go and spy out the lie of the land and the look of the people. After weary days of long tramps, along the surveyed route of the Crow's Nest Rail Road, he made the journey to and fro. On his return came the 'tips and pointers' as he called them; the history of the people and the places; how they had a Moses and an Aaron as licenced lay readers in S. John's Church, Fort Steele one was Low Church and the other was High; how there was jealousy between Fort Steele and Cranhrook; how I could steer my way, safely and successfully, between the Scylla and the Charybdis of the various circumstances on that mission field.

"In the meanwhile, my family had been comfortably ensconced in Rossland. I left them under his paternal care, and proceeded to my chosen mission. After doing parochial duty for some time, I returned for them. And dear 'Father Pat' could not do enough for us.

"We left Rossland, via Northport, for Kaslo; British Columbia, where my household effects were stored, and lo! when ready to start *semper et ubique* 'Father Pat' appeared on the scene. He went with us to Goat's River Landing the temporary port in connection with the new Crow's Nest Rail Road.

"It would be beyond our present scope and intention to describe our journey on a lumber wagon, drawn by four horses, for twenty miles, then in a freight car on a construction train, which was laying rails. Suffice it to say that we reached our mission safely, and through the sound advice which we had received ('To be forewarned is to be forearmed') we found the key to the people and the places.

"As Rector of S. Peter's Church in Revelstoke, British Columbia, sitting quietly in my study, I try to form a just judgment of Mr Irwin's subjective and objective influence what he was to me and what he was to men in general.

"On the one hand, I did not read under him. He was appointed deputy-examiner by the Bishop of New Westminster, and as necessity knows no law, he held the examination in a bedroom of a public-house in Cranbrook. Nevertheless, one could not read the profound volume of his daily life with attention, and not receive great thoughts which sustain the mental and the spiritual life. Thus came.

"'Truths that wake,
To perish never
Which neither listlessness nor mad endeavour
Can utterly abolish or destroy.'

"As Tennyson makes Ulysses say:

"'I am a part of all that I have ever met"

therefore I owe more than I can say to his fond memory. But as a student and a preacher, he left no distinct impression upon me. His great book was human nature, and his best sermon was a pure life. On the other hand, as we consider his objective immortality in men, we may say that he lives and will always live in the memories and affections of the old timers in British Columbia. Characteristic tales are told of him, again and again, in the mines and homes, on the street and in the saloons. And it is a pity that these rich gems of a rare life should be forgotten. A distinct line differentiated him from men in general and priests in particular. Always and only 'Father Pat.' And when we try to sum up we, as children sometimes say when guessing riddles, 'Give it up!' As well try to trace the sunbeams of last summer's sun in every bud and bulb, flower and fruit. Wherever the broad circle of his Catholic life reached, he lives and will live forever. Truly can it be said:

"'His life was gentle; and the elements
So mixed in him that Nature might stand up
And say to all the world: This was a man.'

"And in conclusion:

"'Sir, fare you well;
Hereafter in a better world than this,
I shall desire more love and knowledge of you.'"

Mr Irwin alludes to the writer of the above in the following letter to his Bishop, Dr Dart; and we may see in the whole letter what a bright state of growth and energy pervaded the diocese, active, earnest clergy raising new churches in the rapidly growing townships.

"ROSSLAND CLUB, ROSSLAND, B.C.,
"April, 21st '99.

"MY LORD, I have just returned from Fort Steele and Cranbrook, where I had Easter Communion last Sunday. Procunier is flourishing and has opened a nice church in Fernie the parsonage in Fort Steele is finished.

"There is to be a fast C.P.R. service put on through the Crow's Nest Pass which will save a day nearly. If your Lordship thought of coming in that way, Procunier could meet you at Fernie and he is quite ready for his ordination. I got the 'De fide symbolo' for him. Nelson church is most beautiful and exquisitely finished, and they have it crowded to the doors. Akehurst deserves more than ever he'll get for his almost single-handed labour in getting it up. An ordination and consecration there would be something after your Lordship's heart. Our church committee have consented to take *Festina Lente* as our motto for the present. In my report to the Archdeacon I am showing a year's 'raise' in this parish, and my stipend has almost touched $500; that is a change to the $100 your Lordship referred to as 'a good *beginning*' about two years ago.

"Many thanks for your last letter re the Kootenay Diocese. I think the committee are troubled and troubling about many unnecessary questions.

"Hoping your Lordship will have a good journey out, and that you will soon be with us again, I am, my Lord, your grateful servant, H. IRWIN.

"P.S. My Easter offerings came to $186 which I have easily disposed of."

During the three years of his sojourn at Rossland, Father Pat drew largely too largely on his store of vitality, which seemed inexhaustible. The secret of it all was that he had no desire to live, only to do God's work so long as life should be granted. A friend observes: "He was all over the country, holding services and laying the foundations of a church at Trail, 7 miles east of Rossland, and 2000 feet below, and at Grand Forks and other points in the Boundary, the nearest point being 40 miles over the mountains west of Rossland; two days' journey for most men up and down steep trails, but only one day's for Father Pat, whether on foot or in the saddle.

"His journeys over the mountains were phenomenal; he seemed to be tireless, and he loved the wilds where he was in close touch with Nature; and sometimes to intimate friends he spoke of his frequent sense of the nearness of the Spirit world, with which he seemed in closest touch out on the trails at night."

Anecdotes abound of him at Rossland. One shows his blunt way with the miners, taking them in their own vein: He was a hard football player, and in a match at Nelson, British Columbia, he got a pair of black eyes. Returning to Rossland on Saturday evening, he met a miner in the street, who noted the catastrophe, though his hat was pulled down over his eyes.

"I just stood and looked at him (said the man), and Father Pat came up to me and said, 'What's the matter with you Can't you speak to a man' 'I was just thinking,' said I,' what a pretty pair of eyes those are. Prettiest pair I ever saw.' 'It's not the first time,' said Father Pat. 'Well, you're a nice one for a minister,' said I, 'you're not going to preach with eyes like that?' 'It wouldn't be the first time for that either,' said he. 'Well, I'd be ashamed, if I was you. How did you get 'em?' 'We had a rough game,' he said,' over in Nelson, and I ran up against a fellow, but he's no better off.' "

He preached the next day, but felt bound to make an apology for the eyes.

Another story illustrates the good and bad side of society in Rossland: There was a poor girl who had led an evil life, but in whom Father Pat saw the seeds of better things. Encouraged by him, some young fellows clubbed together to put her in a decent lodging, and to buy a sewing machine with which she might earn an honest living; and this she was sincerely endeavouring to do. A man meeting her in the hotel, greeted her with insulting words. Father Pat happened to be there, and, with his fist in the fellow's face, said:

"You scoundrel, get out of this very quick, or I'll help you out." The man speedily vanished, for the Padre's skill as a boxer was well known.

It was his courage and directness that gave him his influence, though he was no great preacher. Yet he did preach in a most practical way.

One of the finest comments I heard on Father Pat's preaching, was a reply given to a reflection some one made in regard to his pulpit utterances, by a typical old timer.

"Father Pat no preacher? Well, I guess he was right to the point. I'll tell you a story about his preaching.

"There was a young fellow down at Trail very ill. The doctors said there was no salvation for him, he'd got to die, so they sent for Father Pat. He talked to him a bit, and the young chap felt better, and held out his hand and said, 'Thank you, Father Pat; good-bye!' 'Good-bye' said Father Pat, drawing back. 'Good-bye! What do you mean by that? D'ye think I am going anywhere else, but you? I'll say good-night to you if you like; at Doomsday, I'll say good-morning! It's only over the other side of the Divide, and we'll meet together there.' Now that's what I call preaching; brought it all right home to the boy and he died easy."

It is impossible in a memoir like this, compiled from the recollections of many persons, to avoid a certain amount of repetition; and so we need hardly apologize for introducing here one or two extracts from Canadian newspapers. They show as well as anything can, the general feeling about the beloved Padre of the miners.

The first is from the *Toronto Globe*, December 10th, 1898:

"It is something to be part and parcel of a growing country like this. There is, after all, more honour in it than in descent from the men that spurred by William's side when he smote Harold's followers at Hastings. Here at Rossland one pioneer whose career and personality endear him to the Kootenays, and whose memory will ever be a tradition and a blessing. And he is an Episcopalian minister, and an Irishman, the Rev. Henry Irwin. He is known from Fort Steele to Okanagon Landing. There is not a trail through the mountains, nor a road through the valleys, that he has not trudged over and over, and always on errands of mercy and of love.

"He has been the friend and confidant of every pioneer and prospector that has lived in the Kootenays for fifteen years. He saw them come here, poor, eke out a hard existence far from towns and cities and refinement and civilization, but he was always among them with a cheery voice and a kindly smile, and they all loved him, and in pure affection called him 'Father Pat.' He has seen multitudes of his old friends grow rich and famous. He tells of the bacon-and-bean days of the log cabin, and talks kindly of the old friends now dwelling in palatial mansions, and sitting round tables laden with the richest viands and luxuries drawn from every land and clime. But Father Pat prefers the bacon and beans, and hard luck, and black coffee, in the miner's log cabin to the banquet halls of the rich, the great, or the famous. He could have grown rich like others, but he says he wants to be like Him whom he preaches, 'Who had not whereon to lay His head.'

"And thus he 'gangs his gait,' going about doing good with cheerful words and kindly smiles, and a warm clasp of the hand for the Jew and the Gentile, for the orthodox and the heretic, and thus he has won the hearts of the young people who are engaged in upbuilding this glorious young country."

Here is another extract from a local newspaper:?

"Were all the stories of endurance, self-sacrifice and bravery about Father Pat published, it would make an interesting volume. The latest one is very characteristic of him.

"A prospector lay sick away out on the lonely mountain side, thirty miles from doctor or medicine. Father Pat heard of it. He gathered together medicines, and hit the trail. While nearing the cabin, he came across three mounted miners who saluted him with the question, 'Hello, parson, where are you going?' He told them. 'Bill needs a doctor instead of a parson!' They commenced to abuse the minister.

They would not let him pass. Quicker than lightning the parson jerked one of the miners off his horse, knocked another one off, and cleared the trail.

"He reached the sick man's side, and ministered to his wants. On returning the next day he met the three miners, who had camped on the trail bent on revenge. While being abused he appeared meek as a lamb. The trio surrounded him in a threatening manner. Then the parson spoke: 'Will you see fair play if I will fight one at a time?' said he. 'Yes, yes, yes,' exclaimed they, chuckling with delight at the prospect.

"A ring was formed, and soon one of the three measured his length on the ground. 'Come on,' said Father Pat, pleasantly, as the other two seemed somewhat dazed. One came on, and followed the first. 'Next,' said Father Pat. But the third miner took to his heels as though his Satanic Majesty was behind him instead of only a meek minister. The Father bathed the bruises of the two prostrate miners, and after preaching them a sermon on the iniquity of fighting, went on his way."

To complete the series, we have a familiar and friendly letter to a lady, an English friend, to whom Father Pat desired to set forth the real colour and sentiment of his life in the Far West, and we find in it the brightest record of his existence in these latter years. The end was soon to throw its shadow over the story.

"ROSSLAND CLUB,
"Feb. 4, '99.

"DEAR Miss K, Thank you for your kind letter. It's like a breath from a warm land to us, as it's 20 below zero up here just now. Whitest of snowy mountains round us on all sides, and such lovely clear, crisp, clean streets and roads: I think it's the cleanness I like best in winter, though Irish. We are a peculiar very people up here in this sky-bench, 'way up above the clouds and fogs of the lower world, and in a little world of our own; that's a funny wee one. If I could only have snap-shots of the queer people here, I'd make my fortune. There are some 6000 of us here, mostly in shacks, with one good suit of clothes which we wear in the streets and on Sundays, but, as a rule, most rude in speech and dress on the trails.

"I think there's a charm here which people can't get at for some time; and that is, we can be just what we please, what we jolly well like; and we can show it in our speech. Slang answers slang, till we find out who is talking it, and then off we go back to pastures old in the dear old land, and actually talk English, and drop the nasal twang and slang, and become ourselves again. I've studied this carefully, and find that it's only that contrariness, in other nations as well as in my own, which will always put the worst side out at first, till it's sure of its ground. The numbers of languages used here is perplexing.

"I am glad you take an interest in our work. It goes on, on the quiet. We don't talk much, but we can get in and rustle as few can. For instance, we can run a Fancy Fair for a new church for two nights for three hours, and have our $200 worth of stuff, and clear up nearly $2000. That's a fair percentage even out here! We hope to build in spring, but we have to be sure of which way the town will grow. It will not do to have 'Pat's Folly' pointed to as other follies are; and we wait and watch. The most aristocratic portion of our community, named 'the Boys,' put up the present building which is dedicated and known as S. George's Church; but it is but a barn with good furniture in it. Everything from reredos to altar cloths, has been made by the hands of Rosslanders, and we have a very handsome pipe organ fetched in by 'the Boys' too; and so our services are good; our full choral Sunday Celebration often astounds our brethren, and even our Bishops from the other side of the line. But you see we want to be, like all things in a Western camp, more than up to date. The church is lighted by electricity which is brought from fifty miles away, and though it sometimes goes out, it's good light. Just as we began the psalms at evensong a week ago, out it went, and down they sat, and my sermon happened to be on 'darkness,' which lasted till the light came on again, and on we went with the psalms and the service. Little things like that don't even bother us. But though you may think this a flippant kind of letter it's not. I'm only trying to give you an outline of the bench we're on, and the comicalities, so that you can understand the strange position I hold of being licensed by the American Bishop as well as our own, so that I can pray for the President now and then when I've a foot across 'the line.' [As Mr Irwin's duty took him at times across the line dividing Canada from the States, his position was regularized by a license from the American Bishop.] And I glory in proving that the forty-ninth parallel doesn't run through the church, even if it's found in Custom Houses.

"Yes, this mining district has gone on in great strides: little did I think in '85, riding 1200 miles every six weeks to give the scattered people a monthly service from Kamloops, that such a population would be here now, and that we are well within sight of a new Diocese (of Kootenay) under our old Bishop, but with our own Synod. Home Rule! With many thanks for your kind thought. Yours gratefully,

"H. IRWIN."
"Ora pro nobis."

CHAPTER XI
THE PROSPECTOR

WHO has not read "The Sky Pilot," that most picturesque story of life in the Far West By many Father Pat is called "The Sky Pilot," but Arthur Moore was no portrait of Henry Irwin, though some of the details coincide, and the author, "Ralph Connor," allows that there is an aroma of Pat's life and work in the history of the "Sky Pilot." But in "The Prospector," by the same hand, there is a portrait of Irwin in the person of Father Mike, the English clergyman, so hospitable and sympathetic with the young Presbyterian minister, Hamish Macgregor, known as "Shock," who follows his course with power and perseverance. And Shock's reward is to be decreed a failure, and on the lying misrepresentations of some of his blackest sheep, to be withdrawn from his outpost by the Presbyterian Superintendent at head-quarters. The following extract from "The Prospector" illustrates the position with a master-touch:

"'Hello, old man, there's a letter for you in my rooms; thought you'd be in to-day, so took care of it for you.' Father Mike drew near Shock's blackboard and greeted him cordially. 'By Jove! what's the matter with you? What have you been doing to yourself?' he exclaimed, looking keenly into Shock's face.

"' I'm rather seedy,' said Shock, 'played out, indeed '; and he gave Father Mike an account of his last week's experience.

"'Great Caesar!' exclaimed Father Mike, 'that was a close thing. Come right along and stretch yourself out on my couch; a cup of tea will do you good.' Shock, gladly accepting the invitation, went with him. 'There's your letter,' said Father Mike, as he set Shock in his deep armchair; 'you read it while I make tea!'"

And there and then, poor Shock reads the letter from his Convener, enclosing extracts from that of the Superintendent (a sort of Presbyterian Bishop, *Episcopos*, Overseer), stating that Macgregor seems to have failed in tact, and is to be withdrawn at any rate from the Fort, to the more populous and civilized part of his circuit.

"As Shock read the letter, his look of weariness passed away, and the old scrimmage smile came back to his face. 'Read that,' he said, handing the letters to Father Mike, who read them in silence.

"'Withdraw!' he exclaimed, in astonishment when he had finished reading, 'and why, pray? '

"'Oh! don't you see; funds overlapping, denominational rivalry!'

"'Overlapping, rivalry rot! You cannot do my work here, and I cannot do yours. I say, this petition would be rich it if were not so damnable,' added Father Mike, glancing at the document. 'Whereas the town is amply supplied with Church services, there is no desire for services by the Presbyterians, 'or by any others for that matter,' interjected Father Mike. 'Let us see who signs this blessed paper Why, the whole outfit doesn't contribute a guinea a month. Isn't it preposterous a beastly humbug Who is this young whippersnapper, Lloyd, pray' (Naming the chief witness against Shock, at head-quarters.) Father Mike's tone was full of contempt.

"Shock winced. His friend had touched the only place left raw by the letter. 'He is a college friend of mine,' he answered, quickly; 'a fine fellow, and a great preacher.'

"'Oh!' replied Father Mike, drily, 'I beg pardon. Well, what will you do? '

"'Withdraw,' said Shock, simply; 'I haven't made it go, anyway.'

"'Rot!' said Father Mike, with great emphasis. 'Macfarren doesn't want you, and possibly the Inspector shares in that feeling I guess you know why but you are needed in this town, and needed badly.'

"But Shock only replied, 'I shall withdraw; I have been rather a failure, I guess, Let's talk no more about it.'

"'All right, old chap,' said Father Mike, 'come along to tea. I wish to heaven there were more failures like you in the country.' "

This sketch portrait, drawn by a Presbyterian, shows the salient characteristics of Father Pat's nature, the overflowing sympathy, the utter absence of jealousy, the ready hand held out to all downcast or in need of cheering, whether or no they saw eye to eye with himself; the simple kindly hospitality. In the clever story, Shock is the Prospector, searching far and wide for souls to save; but the name might have been given to Father Pat himself, for he was never found resting from the search for souls; and when the community at Rossland had become more civilized, he felt the need of change, and urged his Bishop to send him to some new spot, to unbroken ground. The kindly Bishop saw that he was wearing himself away by incessant work, and by denying himself every comfort, almost every necessary. To and fro he rode on his well-known Indian pony, "Tom," covering more ground than one would think possible; keeping down by incessant labour the ever-gnawing regret for a lost love and a lost life. The Bishop offered him easier work, a lighter post, but he implored to be sent out as a pioneer, and at last he had his way, and was transferred in 1900 to Fairview in the Okanagan district, one of the loveliest parts of lovely British Columbia.

Meanwhile, many things were happening in the diocese. In August 1898, half the city of New Westminster was destroyed by fire, caused by the sparks from a steamer alighting on a heap of straw by the riverside. The wooden houses burned like tinder, and in half an hour a vast extent was on flames. Even the pretty stone church of Holy Trinity, the Cathedral church, was gutted, and in a great measure destroyed. At the time, Bishop Dart was two thousand miles away, on his road to England to plead the cause of his diocese; but in his absence all that was possible was done, Government sent aid, and in two years' time, the church arose from Us ashes, a very well-proportioned and dignified edifice, completed in 1904 by a tower. It is interesting to compare Holy Trinity Church as it now is, with the first little log church in the wilderness built by the present Bishop of Norwich.

The number of clergy had doubled, organisations were multiplying (though not too fast, for Bishop Dart has always preferred quality to quantity in church work), and there was already a feeling that the vast diocese needed subdivision, and that such subdivision was possible, though as yet (even though the finances of the diocese had somewhat improved) there was but a meagre income for one Bishop little over £500 a year and no prospect of any for a second Bishop in Kootenay. But the thing had to be done, and done it was in time. The Kootenay or eastern district, where Rossland and Fairview lie, is now (1909) fully equipped with its own Synod, its own Archdeacon, but under the same Bishop, Dr Dart, who felt that it was easier for him to undertake the journey of 1000 miles to Kootenay to hold the Synod at Nelson, than for all the Kootenay clergy to spend their time and money in coming to a Synod at New Westminster. The following is Mr Irwin's answer to the Bishop's invitation to join a Committee on the subject of the new diocese, to meet at Nelson:

"FAIRVIEW, B. C., [Fairview is situated in the famous Okanagan valley, about 28 miles south of Penticton, which is reached by the Canadian Pacific Railway. It is the leading Free Milling Gold Camp in British Columbia.]

"Aug. 3rd, 1900.

"MY LORD, Thank you for your kind letter. I shall be glad to be of use to your Lordship in any way, and shall be proud to act on the Executive Committee. But do you think I am likely to attend any meetings. It's far further from the end of track here than people think it: a long day's long journey.

"However, I thank your Lordship for the honour conferred, and shall be glad to hear you have put some more central man, like Hedley, on the Committee. I feel that I could not, in any truth, say that I should like to go to Revelstoke, even if I had not my pet work on hand here. I guess, my Lord, that you have heard some yarns of my poverty-stricken aspect in overalls! but that's my way parabolic, and I think you must be the receptacle for some of the many yarns started on me and my work up here, by people who know nothing of the facts or the country; ahead of track we don't expect much 'style,' and I wear overalls, therefore I must be poverty-stricken, is the false logic. I have all I need and more, and have lots of good friends who are only too kind to me. If your Lordship will let me go ahead quietly here for a year or so, I think we shall have a strong body of good Church people. I should despise the man who would drop the plough just because of some rocky ground: and I get all the meals I want.

"Mr Robins was introduced to some camping out a little time ago, and I fancy he thought it a little rough under a tree in saddle-blankets! With many thanks for your Lordship's kindness and thought for me, I am, your Lordship's humble servant,

"H. IRWIN."

We read between the lines, and see in this letter certain symptoms of the trouble that was creeping over the heroic missionary. Tales of his self-denial and probable overstrain had reached the ears of the Bishop, who had delicately hinted at the need of more care and comfort, if illness were to be averted. But in the unwonted hesitation to bestir himself:" Do you think I am likely to attend meetings a long day's journey;" and "if your Lordship will let me go quietly ahead here for a year or so," we note a change in Father Pat's view of life, which was before a longing for perpetual motion; no day was too long, no ride too hard for him.

The Rev. W. A. Robins here mentioned (now Vicar of Cirencester) came out for five years' service, and nobly attacked the difficulties of rough pioneer work; earned the affection and respect of all, erected a mission hall at Greenwood, was able to live on the stipend supplied by his congregation without diocesan aid, and at the end of his five years, left behind him a sorrowing flock and a record of admirable work.

Two anecdotes illustrative of Father Pat's methods forcible and effective! come to us from the short sojourn at Fairview. Among a crowd of miners, one coarser than the rest and not quite sober, ventured to insult the Padre, who paid no attention to him till words were added which were an insult to religion and to our Lord Himself. Then Father Pat turned on him fiercely, saying: "I don't mind your insulting me, but you shall not insult my Master."

The miner drawing nearer, dared Father Pat to prevent him, expecting that his own superior bulk would give him the advantage over the parson. But after a further warning, Irwin turned on the man, using his fists scientifically, as he well knew how to do, and punished him severely. In the end, the man went down like a log, unconscious and bleeding. Down on his knees beside him went Father Pat, anxiously examining his injuries, and then and there in a fit of remorse he cried: "O Lord, forgive me for not telling this poor man that I was a champion boxer at Oxford."

The other story tells how Father Pat came wheeling his little portable organ with intent to hold a service in the boarding-house and saloon for miners near West Fork, Kettle River. The proprietor of this extremely rough hotel was one Cook, a well-known "character," Irish, like Father Pat himself, and not unwilling to let his saloon be used for the simple service to which the popular parson managed to attract a good many of the miners. The service commenced, and was listened to with attention, as Father Pat's services and sermons always were, because the men all knew him to be "white" (their expressive word of praise, meaning honourable, manly and straightforward). But when the time came for the hymn, generally the favourite part of the service, and when the tune had been played through on the little organ, lo! no voice responded, and there was silence. A leader was lacking. Father Pat was no vocalist, and all the men were shy. After repeated but vain exhortations to the men to tune up, Father Pat turned to his friend Gorman West, who stood by him, exclaiming, "Gorman, you beggar, sing!" West replied, "Well, Pat, if I sing, every other son of a gun will walk out!" "For Heaven's sake then, don't I" rejoined Father Pat, and closed the service without a hymn.

Do these anecdotes seem trivial or profane or beside the mark. They are necessary to show the tone of the picture; and indeed those who have been in the Far West can easily realize that such freedom from formality means no irreverence. If irreverence be meant, there is no doubt about it! The language then excludes all misinterpretation.

One more of Father Pat's bright letters to a friend in England remains to us; but in it we can trace the overstrain, a certain physical shrinking from the hardships which in former days were salt to the life of the missionary. The poor earthly body cannot be misused for ever; in the end it revolts against the severity with which ascetics and enthusiasts treat it, and abruptly ends the scene.

"FAIRVIEW, B.C.
"Aug. 14th, 1900.

"DEAREST B. Just got in from an eight days' trip on 'the camel,' that will show you what 'tough' means. After A.M. service here last Sunday week I did forty-one miles between 1 P.M. and 7 P.M. for P.M. service that's not bad for an old crock of a horse then on and up the Kettle River, another forty miles, and away back off trails into the forest some thirty more miles by Wednesday, when on came one of those awful rainfalls we have in summer, cold as charity, even colder, and one's light gum coat is no protection; nor would tarpaulin keep out the soak one gets from the brush as you fight your way in and out of deer-trail windings, cutting with your axe a tree here and a big branch there, to give the horse a hole to crawl through. How one could ever find one's way back except for the 'blazes' on the trees would puzzle a Quaker; but on a horse here you need never think of how to get back, as the horse does all the thinking in such case. Three to four miles away through the very depth of a thick pine forest, in and out of the thickets of underbrushed deer coverts and lots of deer too to look at *on a wet day*, with a shirt and pants and socks and boots and straw hat and nothing more on, will give you my feelings with nothing to eat but some chocolate and a lump of cheese from Wednesday 7 A.M. till Thursday 9 A.M., in the saddle the whole time, then into camp where the tents were the only dry places, as fires have no roofs, so had to roll up in a saddle blanket and rig a gum coat over one's things in front of the fire so as to get 'em dry. There's a bit of a trip for you! I think the one thing that makes it so 'winsome' is the fact that away there in the forests you are alone in places seldom trodden by the foot of man. To pursue my way: next night found me out on the heights of the summits, on a vile bad trail, tracking back to this place, some sixty miles; about dark I struck a tent of two Rosslanders lost in the mountains, with whom I stayed to give them the last items of war news, etc. I wish I had a snapshot of the old waggon spread for that was the tent! under which lay the two owners side by side, and I, at the mouth across their feet, slept as guard with a great fire of logs three feet high blazing on to the graceful scene! Then up at 3 A.M. to hunt for the horses, which had to huddle together under some thick brush of willows, so that it took an hour to track them, as the bears in these parts scare the life out of horses at nights, and mountain lions lie for them, so that a rock or black stump is a *bête noire*. Off then and away at 4 A.M. and twenty miles to breakfast, leaving the pair snoring under their roof and the night's fire just dying out in smoking gasps.

"Those fellows *were* glad to see me, as they had used their last match.

"Then another day of forty miles and back here to get to a bed again, with the old whitey 'Tom' as fit as a fiddle, glad to get out of the wild mountains to those ranges again. I wish you were here with me for the deer and birds. My! but those big mountain grouse are whoppers; they are as big as a Brahma fowl; and when they blow out peacocky-wise to guard their young, they look like a great Chinese fan with a bird's eyes and bill stuck in the centre and a little pair of bird's claws gummed on below; and such colours too! The golden Oriole is the only other to beat them. So long, B. Yours in love,

"PAT."

CHAPTER XII
THE END

THE end now drew rapidly near. Things were rather bad in Fairview Camp; business black, the clergyman's income from his impoverished flock very slender indeed; and we may be sure that if he had a loaf and a pot of tea, everyone was welcome to share it. The letter, dated November 21, 1900, addressed to the Bishop, tells its own tale:

"FAIRVIEW, B.C.
"Nov. 21st, 1900.

"MY LORD, I should have answered your last, but I have been waiting to hear some news which will either make or break this camp. This Fairview Corporation has now a deal on in New York, and upon it depends the future of this place. At present in this warm southern valley we have four below zero, and things are very quiet. I just manage to live, and that's all, on what collections I can get. Penticton is my safety and stay in these hard times. I don't know how to thank your Lordship for the $25 a month you have so kindly let me have for the whole year. It is quite impossible for a man to live here and work Penticton without a grant; but perhaps in the spring things will have taken a turn for the better. There are not more than ten of our own church people here! But we get about forty or fifty in church. I try to keep the services going in as many places as I can, but it's hard this winter time: no wonder the Kirk have no students out in the hard months of the year!

"I am always glad to be in hard places, and I hope the development this next year will make both Fairview and Penticton very important.

"I fancy the new roads from twenty mile Camp and from Princetown will make Penticton a very large place.

"With my most grateful Christmas wishes. I am, my Lord, yours humbly,

"H. IRWIN."

So things went on. The Bishop, realizing that the pathetic silence of this brave worker covered a depth of tragic suffering, urged him to take a rest, and to go home to his friends in Ireland for a time. At length, after considerable persuasion, Mr Irwin consented to do so; and it was arranged that after a rest at home and on his return to British Columbia, he should act as an itinerant missionary to the wilder districts where it was impossible to keep a settled clergyman. In a new country such districts abound. Men come out and establish themselves as ranchers far from civilization or "the sound of the church-going bell." They need space and pasture for their herds of cattle, and discourage others from settling near them on this account. Yet it is bad for them to live these lonely lives; they often deteriorate in character, or become morbid, and suicide too often ends the sad tale. To such men, the visits of a Father Pat would have been invaluable. To the northern districts of Cariboo and Chilcoten he would have ridden from time to time four or five days' hard riding; settlers ten, twenty, thirty miles apart, separated by streams, precipices, forests. Even yet the problem is unsolved, and the Bishop is appealing for funds and men for this special work. [The opening of the new North Trans-Continental Railway will open up these parts and aid Church work.]

For Father Pat it was not to be. "The Lord had need of him" in Paradise. It seemed to many that the fine gold of his mind was become dim, and that there was a partial clouding of the intellect. He set off for England at the end of 1901. No one knows what befel, for he did not tell the tale. But it is surmised that he got out of the train some distance before reaching Montreal, resolving to walk on: or as is said in Dr Kingston's letter, "he resolved to go for a long country walk."

In British Columbia, with its clear, light, milder climate, he had slept out of doors in all seasons, and loved to do so. But in Montreal, in mid-winter, this cannot be done. Heat and cold are far more intense in Eastern Canada. Had he been in full possession of his faculties, Father Pat would have known this; but he seems to have lain down under the stars, half unconscious, and thus the bitter cold did its sad work.

We recall Father Mackonochie lying dead under the leafless trees of the Scotch Highlands, watched by the two faithful dogs of his friend Chinnery Haldane; with the snow drawn over his face like a veil from an angel's hand. Truly there was a likeness in the end of these two heroes of our Church.

The details were given verbally by the Mother Superior of Notre Dame Hospital at Montreal to one who has kindly communicated them to us.

One morning early in January 1902, a farmer driving along the Sault au Recollet Road, a few miles from Montreal, saw a man walking with difficulty on the frozen ice. It seemed to him as if the man were pushing his feet on, rather than lifting them up. The farmer immediately ran to him and asked if he were ill, or if his feet were frozen. The pedestrian replied that he did not feel any pain, but a numbness in the legs. The farmer kindly took him in his sleigh and drove him to a physician living at the Sault. After examination, the doctor administered a cordial to the stranger, who refused to give his name, and told the farmer to drive him as quickly as possible to a hospital in Montreal, and the stranger begged that it might be that of Notre Dame, which is famous for its nursing.

When there, he refused to give any name but, "William Henry," and the Sisters let it pass. His clothing had no clerical feature about it, and he took from the lining of his cap a package of letters and banknotes. The shoes had to be cut from his feet, so hardly were they frozen; and the feet were soaked in a medical preparation to thaw them. Tears ran down the cheeks of the nursing Sisters, as they knew the agony that was but beginning; but Father Pat (for it was he) joked with his nurses, and said their tears affected him more than the pain. His wit, his kindness, his elevated ideas and courteous manners convinced the doctors and nurses that their patient was a gentleman, and an uncommon one. For some days Father Pat felt scarcely any pain. Mortification had set in; but he did not seem to realize his position. His appetite was good, his mind clear and admirable; there seemed to be a magnetic current attracting to him all those who had access to his room. After the first day the Superioress went to him and said he had forgotten to give his full name when arriving, and that she was ready to register it if he would kindly tell what it was. With a lurking, wistful look Father Pat said that "women were never satisfied, and always curious beyond measure," and changed the topic; but the Sister reiterated her question, saying that she was morally sure that "William Henry" was not his name, at least not all his name. Then Father Pat said that she was right, and that he wanted to see the house doctor of the hospital, who was Sir William Kingston's son. Dr Kingston used to have several daily pleasant chats with Father Pat, and came to his bedside in a moment. Their conference was long. Mr Irwin entrusted his letters, papers, and his name to Dr Kingston, on the condition that he would not divulge the addresses of the envelopes nor his name before his death. During the days when Father Pat was comparatively well he entertained those near him brightly, wittily and cleverly upon many topics, sometimes talking of the West, but he never pronounced the name of any place, nor would he give any clue to his name or calling.

After the third day the throat became affected; there was difficulty in swallowing and in articulation, and now for the first time the sufferer seemed to realize his position. He asked the Sisters if it was the end, and on their answering that it was, he gave them a long, sad look.

The Reverend Canon Wood, Vicar of S. John's, Montreal, had often visited Father Pat in the Hospital, the Sisters having sent for him as soon as they knew that their mysterious visitor belonged to the Church of England. He was now sent for, and for the next three days he was often with the sufferer, who seemed relieved and cheered by his presence. His sufferings were borne to the end with the utmost patience; but, a few hours before death, he became delirious.

During Father Pat's stay at the Hospital two police officers had called to see him, to obtain his name, and to question him; but this the Mother Superior firmly opposed, and the officials yielded to her decree that the dying man should be left in peace.

Quietly at last, as a child, the missionary yielded up his soul to God, keeping his secret to the end and wrapping his broken heart, his weary spirit, in the dignity of silence.

It was at one time reported that before his death Mr Irwin became a member of the Church of Rome; but it was not so. The nursing Sisters indignantly denied it. They do not proselytize, but respect the religion of their patients.

His body was removed for burial by Canon Wood, and the facts being now revealed by Dr Kingston, the remains were conveyed to Sapperton, New Westminster, to be laid beside those of his wife and child.

From a letter by Dr Kingston we extract the following:

"At all times he hid with a smile the sufferings he must have experienced, and his pluck and unselfishness were remarkable." He would suffer agony rather than awake an attendant at night to get a glass of water or anything he needed.

"His papers were given to me in a sealed envelope (continues Dr Kingston), addressed to a friend in Ireland. We ignored his address or the fact that he was the well known Father Pat. Probably his reason for so doing was to prevent me cabling to his family, or from informing his numerous friends in Montreal of his condition.

After a severe operation on the throat, to prevent suffocation, when the power of speech had passed away, he signed for pencil and paper, and wrote: "That was what was needed, but it was hard." During the night (says Dr Kingston) I was twice called to see him; the second time, as I reached the door, he beckoned me to come back, and when I returned shook hands with me. His breathing became easier; and towards morning he lost consciousness, and towards midday, January 13th, he died without having regained his senses.

"For my own part, I have never seen so much strength and so much gentleness combined."

(Signed) "D. A. KINGSTON."

When in Montreal I was admitted to the presence of the Rev. Canon Wood, so well known as "Father Wood," Vicar of S. John's Church. Montreal. He is one of the best known and most highly revered Anglican clergy in the whole Dominion, beloved by all without distinction of sect; and in his life, simple and ascetic as Henry Irwin himself. In the dim, half-lighted church, where the choir were practising in his presence, and where the great Rood over the screen seemed to spread a hallowing shadow, there we found the venerable priest, who took us to the vestry and told us how he had ministered to Henry Irwin on his deathbed; how his loving Christian character had shone through the veils of physical pain and mental beclouding. "And certainly," said Father Wood, "he died as he had lived, in the faith of the English Church, though others have made statements to the contrary. Were it otherwise, would not the Roman Church have claimed the right to interment"

We left the place with a profound thankfulness that on his deathbed the noble missionary was not alone. Though with the instinct of hiding his innermost feelings from men, which seems to have been always his characteristic, yet he was not alone in the passing hour. "Not alone" truly, for his Lord was with him; and also there were the loving tender ministrations of the large-hearted Sisters, and beside his bed stood a faithful priest. Of Henry Irwin we may say that in life and death he was such as Jesus owns for His true disciple and a pastor of His flock, one who could point the way through suffering to glory.

"Christe's lore and His Apostles' twelve
He preached; but first he followed it himself."

CHAPTER XIII
MEMORIALS

No sooner did the news that Father Pat was no more reach British Columbia, than the wish arose in the whole community that he should be buried among them. The coffin was placed in the Cathedral Church of New Westminster, where crowds of people came to pay the last sad tribute of respect. On a lovely afternoon, among many friends, he was laid at rest in the pretty cemetery on the hillside, by the wife he loved so fondly.

"It will be many a long day before his name is forgotten, and his unselfish devotion shall cease to live as an influence for good in the grateful memory of many a miner and railwayman in British Columbia." ["The New Era."]

A subscription list was at once opened for a memorial to Father Pat. "The miners vied with one another in their desire to honour the best friend and benefactor they ever had. An ambulance was purchased for the use of miners in and around Rossland, and so, though being dead, he yet speaketh in the cure of sickness and the relief of suffering."

A monument was also erected to his memory. It stands in the main street of Rossland. It combines the uses of a lamp and a drinking fountain, and speaks to the people mutely of the Light that their friend humbly followed, and of the Water of Life from which he strove to give them to drink.

The inscriptions on the monument are as follows:
On the face of it are these words:

"Rich he was of holy thought and work."

In loving memory of
REV. HENRY IRWIN, M.A. (OXON),
First Rector of S. George's Church, Rossland.

Father Pat: A Hero of the Far West

Affectionately known as Father Pat.
Obiit, January 13th, 1902,

Whose life was unselfishly devoted to the welfare of his
fellowmen irrespective of creed or class.

"His home was known to all the vagrant train; He chid their
wanderings, and relieved their pain."

And on each side of the same stone fountain are these shorter
inscriptions:

On the East: "I was thirsty, and ye gave Me to drink."

On the West: "I was an hungered, and ye gave Me to eat."

On the North: "In Memoriam, Father Pat."

"He who would write an Epitaph for thee,
And do it well, must first begin to be
Such as thou wert. For none can truly know
Thy life, thy worth, but he that liveth so."

On the South: "A man he was to all the country dear."

These inscriptions, chosen with such tender care, show that this
memorial was no mere show, but one that was meant to express the
love in the hearts of the donors.

Close by is another memorial, perhaps as eloquent and even more
touching: A cairn or pyramid erected to Father's Pat's memory by
the miners themselves, consisting of specimens of all the rich and
valued ores produced by the mines of Rossland; each in its own
division and labelled with the name of the mine.

How can we sum up this record of a sensitive spirit, reserved to
excess as to its inmost treasures; true to the core; tender, unselfish
and self-forgetting. Unconventional, yes, to a high degree; one not to

be measured by the common standards of men but with "the measure of an angel," and to be fitly appraised only by those beings who surround us invisible and regard us "With larger other eyes than ours."

REQUIESCAT IN PACE.

Lightning Source UK Ltd.
Milton Keynes UK
UKHW010252110719
345909UK00001BA/187/P